MW01283624

I don't need no pimp
Nor chief of police
To tell me when to love

—Nicole Zach
"Sex Law"

THE RUTHERFORD RED WHEELBARROW
Number 10, 2017
©2017 RED WHEELBARROW POETS
All rights revert to authors.
ISBN: 978-1-387-13079-5
ORDER MORE COPIES: Lulu.com, Amazon.com
VISIT OUR WEBSITE:
https://redwheelbarrowpoets.org

EDITOR: Jim Klein
MANAGING EDITOR: Mark Fogarty
MANAGING EDITOR: John Barrale
MANAGING EDITOR: Melanie Klein
ONLINE EDITOR: Wayne L. Miller
COVER COLLAGE: Janet Kolstein
DESIGNER: Claudia Serea
COLLAGE and LINE DRAWINGS: Janet Kolstein, Don Zirilli

Thanks to our generous financial contributors!

WHITE CHICKENS PRESS
PO Box 1691, Rutherford, NJ 07070

POETRY

PROSE

PAMELA HUGHES on the Meadowlands; the RWB on the Internet by WAYNE L. MILLER; ARTHUR RUSSELL and JOHN J. TRAUSE on WCW; book reviews by MARK FOGARTY; an interview of JIM KLEIN by LOREN KLEINMAN; and CONTRIBUTORS.

Kolstein

poetry

Illustrations by Don Zirilli appear on pages 30, 42, 71, 81, 83, 88, 110, 122, 142, 164, 193, 209, 223, 232 and 238.

WHITE CHICKENS PRESS

The Rutherford Red Wheelbarrow Poets Anthology
The Red Wheelbarrow Numbers 2 to 10

THE RUTHERFORD POETRY SERIES

Blue Chevies	**JIM KLEIN**
To Eat Is Human, to Digest Divine	**JIM KLEIN**
A Dress Full of Holes	**KATHY KUENZLE**
From the Sounds of Chewing	**GEORGE PERENY**
Absence Implies Presence	**MICHAEL O'BRIEN**
Shakespeare's Moths	**JOHN BARRALE**
Zerilda's Chair	**GEORGE DeGREGORIO**
Myshkin's Blues	**MARK FOGARTY**
Peninsula	**MARK FOGARTY**
Phantom Engineer	**MARK FOGARTY**
Sun Nets	**MARK FOGARTY**
Continuum: The Jaco Poems	**MARK FOGARTY**
The Tall Women's Dance	**MARK FOGARTY**

Available from Amazon.com and Lulu.com

FEATURED POET: JANET KOLSTEIN

JANET KOLSTEIN

Born in Bloomfield, NJ, Kolstein received a BA Degree in Fine Arts from Montclair State College and worked as a texile designer in Manhattan's garment center while painting at night and week-ends in a studio on Fourteenth Street. Her artworks were exhibited at various venues in New York. In 1987, she was involved in a near-fatal road traffic accident in Ireland that changed the course of her life. Now living in Guttenberg, NJ, she contributes artwork to shows throughout the U.S. Her poems have appeared in the Fall 2006/Winter 2007 and 2012 edition of *LIPS, The Poetry of Place: North Jersey in Poetry* (2008), *The Rutherford Red Wheelbarrow* collections 2-10, *The Newsead Abbey Byron Society Review* (2009) and *Instigatorzine* (2104). Kolstein's computer-aided artwork is featured on *The Rutherford Red Wheelbarrow* covers (2013 and 2017), and she contributed illustions for *The Red Wheelbarrow 9* (2016). (Photo by Natalie Robbins)

Can It Be the Weekend, Again?

The trash-filled rush to question
my pedestrian escape plan
mocked the force of life's
bite wounds.

Am I tough enough for the marathon?

Each narrative in my head has a terminal
with a thousand disappointments pulling in,
and phrases, winking with praises,
pulling out.

A full-length masterpiece seems more fictional
than not,
and a vanishing point puts perspective
in storytelling
that goes above and beyond arithmetic.

Now, each day I wake to a lot of pressure
to flip the hourglass by my bed.

There is no substitute for an amulet
to deceive yourself.

In the waiting booth
with two black suitcases
smelling of cough syrup and bleach,
I search for safety
when my face gets hot—

high tech, low voltage,
visible light heavier than helium—
something, anything,
to fill the spectered lot.

The Bright and Shadow Years

When The City was new to me,
I swung Chagall-like through the streets
as if strangers were accessories
to my fantasy.

Sometimes, I was a lonely mouse
in a Twinkie factory,
hustling around the pine floors
for crumbs and a foothold
in the post-industrial door.

I had to find a job, a new job,
a society of apple-picking experts,
a hand-painted company of cards,
an historic date, fleshy and ripe.

Pay phones reached their pinnacle.
Go-sees and *meet me's*
with cherry-red canticles,
a libertine's sewer breath
perfumed as ambition.

Invaders flashing smiles
were unsure of what to do,
leaning into the gilded lanes
on the oily fluid of rapid change.

How is it after years spent running
for a bus, a taxi, a subway,
a dollar, a dime, a dream,
I finally became concerned
with the pace of my slow ascent,
and barely even made a dent
in the vaulted ceiling?

Can a Secret Keep a Secret

when it feeds on your blood
like a fat tick
that won't let go?

When it flies under the radar
on a lost track,
Mephisto jams with The Friar
on Juliet's baby grand.

It's an old manuscript
pulled from prison,
hard candy from a cloud,
a vagabond in the underworld.

If you sledgehammered your secret
at a county fair,
how high would it rise on the meter?
Is its import a Fata Morgana
in the marshland of your mind?

Sometimes, that door knocker
drops to your gut like a whetstone.

The secret is the reason you still have a job,
your spouse,
the love of your fans,

why all the joys in life
have learned to play
professional chess,

and a prophet
conquers people
with a smile.

Who Are You Wearing?

Click! Click!   Click! Click!
   Click!   Click! Click!
Click!   Click!Click! Click!   Click!
Can you get more love than this?

Blown-out blond hair in a blunt cut
swings around her golden head
with every pivot.

To the cry of her name,
she twirls
towards and away from
anonymous mortals
like me
watching tv.

Her hand-spangled gown
shimmers
with every swish and sway
of her Cannes camera-ready body,

and I wanna feel
le tapis rouge under my feet,
to soak up what was meant to be
mine,
to toast the week-end gross
from a thousand screens
launched in my honor,
my face a shrine,
bankable!
riding high on flash
and flesh,
Valium to calm the riptide.

Kiss-kiss
(don't touch my air-brushed lips)
before the bling
goes back
in the box.

Zarafa

She sailed down the Nile
far, far away from her home
and across the Mediterranean Sea—
Africa behind her, Marseille ahead,
the first giraffe ever seen in France.

A sight of wonder and delight
the moment her hooves touched land,
she walked to Paris to be
another *jeune fille*
in the king's menagerie
in the *Jardin des Plantes.*

A star, an oddity,
alone in captivity,
she would live out her life
among the hundreds of thousands
who came to stare
and buy wares with her likeness.

Was there a man, woman, or child
who pitied her plight,
looked into her unguarded gaze and wondered
if giraffes can dream of herds on savannas,
of other long necks to nibble
and twine?

A gift from Muhammed Ali Pasha to King Charles X, Zarafa ("lovely one") landed in Marseille on October 1826 and inspired "giraffemania" until becoming passe. She died in 1845.

A Stream of Alluring Things That Don't Really Exist

Something raw and natural whirls
around the bedroom walls,
veined with deep blue, baby blue,
the blue of Naples Bay,
the blue of a jay.

There is no curse
in the fevered dreams of marble and alabaster,
timeless as light that streams though a rainbow.

Austin's sleek young physique,
leather and wood smoke
knit together crazy talk about matchups
and fans who smile louder
and play ball with punch.

They were all magically turned on—
drunken jet-lagged dancers in cowboy boots
ready to service every piece of art.

Couples were mirrors of desire,
buttery objects that slid
up and down against each other
into pools on the floor.

Such behavior is a form of surveillance
when *just trust us* isn't enough,
and dubious lust,

a totem stained black,
ensures an absence of questions.

Walking such a fine line,
you have to live here to understand
their playground is a giant round bowl of music
open to the sky,

and contenders, hot or cold,
are sparkly, leopard-covered runners
twirling ritual above their heads.

Pound of Poems

I wish the piano
could gun the engine
under the hood,
and the choir could
raise the roof on
a fortress of words.

I wish the drums
could pound out
a pound of poems
without spilling
a drop of blood.

Let the theremin
quiver in my hands,
shaping a heart
with a dagger
written in it.

Snow Is Falling

on my parents' boxed-up bones
moldering in their cold-case files.

Snowflakes are falling softly,
not on Joyce's "crooked crosses,"
but on cars and roofs—
shades of Grandma Moses,
and Hiroshige, too.

Peering down from my window,
I see a lone pioneer
laying claim to virgin snow.

Tow-trucks blink their welcome brights
with the season's festive lights,
and some drivers have to brave the icy roads
for reasons I can just suppose.

Blizzards used to be fun
when I flirted with the wicked winds
and made angels under the cold sun.
I didn't scan the winterscape
and think of broken hips.

Snowflakes are softly falling
on the streets and on the river,
sticking to one,
becoming the other.

A Night at Lucky Cheng's

The drag queens can't make us blush.
Laugh, yes—blush, no.

We've danced with the devil
and the horse he rode in on.

We've held hands with the dead
and made soup with eye of newt.
Fresh and dried.

No lip-syncing, hash-slinging queen
can embarrass us now.
We know the transformative powers of make-up.
We're familiar with nipping and tucking.
We remember the pinch of high-heels, girdles and wigs.

Our desires wander the night
in staid celebration,
as we lift our slush to the mighty art
of tart self-creation.

Say It

It didn't look good for my father,
and we both knew his options had shrunk
to the size of an atom.
Walking me out to the car,
he lingered in the crisp night air
wanting to speak.

I looked over at the hardened dirt,
Where, underground
bulbs banked their ripening color.

For the first time I could remember,
my father said *I love you.*

I put my hand on his arm,
his heavy sleeve,
while our breath vaporized in fragile puffs.

He needed to know if I would be all right.
Unmarried and crippled.
Had he been a good father?

In a moment,
years were wiped clean
and I told him I'd been happy.

Say it, you stubborn mule,
say "I love you" back.

Why couldn't I say it?

The question folded in on itself
like an origami crane,

and ruminating on the tangle
of dying roots,
drove away.

Run

When summer's satisfaction
sucks on the juice
and spits out the seeds,
and flowers turn
brown around the edges,

my pulse says run,
run to your lover
waiting for you,

watching by the window,
waiting for you
to appear at his door.

So run to your lover
when days melt in the heat,
and flies commit suicide
in sugary drinks.

Take a taxi to your lover
fermenting in hops
as dusk fades
and the park turns black
with shadows.

My pulse says go, go,
run for the bus
spewing hot fumes,
and don't mind the sweat
that opens your pores,

you'll be writhing and wet
next to your lover
who's waiting,

waiting to take you
on the other side.

Looking for a Poem

I'm looking for a poem
that hangs in a cluttered closet
holding on to frayed ideals,
tattered notions that no longer fit,
and reeking of the perfume of the past.

I'm looking for a poem
that stumbles through the night
unwashed and snarling,
carrying a case of perception
and a bottle of forgetfulness
when the time comes for sleeping—
a poem that tastes so good
you go back for seconds—

words Tebaldi-big and *tremolando,*
like *fragrant frangipani* and *zaftig Aphrodite*
sweetening the tongue
without the aftertaste of *wolfbane*—

a poem that lumbers like a bear
through the woulds, shoulds and coulds,
past the sanctimonious sentries
and usurpers of dreams—
one that won't lie, pussyfoot or pander—
a poem, raving and delirious,
that can yodel, tap dance, juggle fire.

Good, Clean Fun: Jan Nemec's Obituary Reconstructed

Filmed with a clarinet,
Mr. Nemec once told an interviewer
of a series of formally inventive sadistic games
while trying to steal his glamorous past
and a loaf of bread.
Under duress, he managed to complete "Martyrs of Love"
which brought him to the attention of unwitting characters
on their way to a garden party.
He found himself in thrall to up-and-coming directors
plotting a short film about his alma mater, strange scenes
and even stranger people.

The film, which he returned to the Czech Republic,
explores a hymn to the drastic situations
of the new Czech cinema in Amsterdam.
An autobiographical short story ended in divorce.
He was invited to run afoul by his first wife.
Quickly, he played out a third feature on the screen
and made videos with three prisoners
being transported from the New York Film Festival in 1968.
Rolling through the streets of Prague,
he was permitted to interpret the emotions
of a Nazi train, "dream realism,"
and his practical father.
After being barred, with farcical overtones,
from one concentration camp to another,
Jan Nemec blocked government censors
and made several films for television
through no fault of his own.
He was born with a hand-held camera,
and on July 12, 1936, he played piano until dissuaded
to assess the meaning of his striving.
He made the documentary, *A Report on Pearls With My Mother,*
in which human beings told the tragicomic story
of a comedy based on his life.
Showcasing a bleak landscape,
with financing from a Dutch film company,
he employed a style he called "good, clean fun,"
straining his relationship with a jazz musician.
He returned to American audiences,
which consisted of two elderly residents at a clinic.
The German government,
at one another's throats,
confirmed his death at 79.
A daughter had to be smuggled out of the country
and did not give a cause.

Gigi's Garden

Gigi's garden was worthy of legend—
100 years of temples and dragons,
idols and illusions,
harmony and hum,
a sunlit journey blending
the stillness and chaos
of wildflowers among the woods.

Abandoned in the winter frost
to a Utopia of ghosts,
cedars float
like caftans of chiffon,
and opera coats
shot through with golden threads
were hung on evergreens.

A blue-blooded saint
could try to rule a forest
of bergamot and power,
a rustic essence
discreetly clad
in a crown of sage.

With my flea-market eyes,
I saw old-fashioned photographs
dusted in a warm patina,
like a shady grove hanging in midair.

Arteries

The turnpike of the eternal flame
exudes an essence that scratches the air
and courses through the veins.

But how clean the snowy egret looks
against the marsh's vegetation
that abuts the exit ramp
leading to 280.

As I roll towards the tollbooth,
an incoming plane roars
over a passel of cars
and symmetrically lands
under the pilot's silken hand.

Coins in the metal catcher
ring a hollow *THANK YOU*.

In her Elizabethan ruff of silver-blue,
the Fornasetti moon frowns
on my hands clenching the wheel.

Loneliness and fear have come along for the ride,
but the only way to get anywhere
is drive.

Tea Leaves

After an Afghan dinner of chanting and weeping,
our special guest read tea leaves,
and, with uncanny skill,
endowed a legacy
on each unspoken quest.

The out-of-touch hostess mixed *anime*
with mangos and music,
and we felt secure in an odd way,
trusting the supply chain
to make the world safe again
for secret domains
where handmaidens rose
from the half-frozen shadows.

What can I know
rambling through fairy-tale meadows,
haunted by the hourglass
running full blast?

From the lessons of my heyday,
I drew on tales of mothers who flew
at hunters of gold-plated street food
and unicorns who danced
to the strains of bagpipes.

When the wheels on my mountain bike
couldn't be repaired,
I had to embrace that omen
and coax a puny, but precious, glow
out of a handful
of tedious woe.

Humors

The news from the city of sound
hasn't been good,
but sometimes, hey,
you have to swallow your pride
to make a dream come true.

I dreamt of monkey milk,
dancing with a broken heel
and hanging out with the druggies
when all four humors
started leaking from my eyes
and I needed to look at ruins—

paint peeling from clapboard skins
and shutters banging in the wind.

They showed me a photo of the grounds
near the shell of mom and pop's
where it grows all weedy,
but spring moved in with her greenery,
and the residents, rooted to the place,
fluffed out their emerald afros
looking as good
as they ever did.

Talking to a Poster on the Wall

The inner circle
says everything is normal.
Your brain is playing
tricks on you.

Semi-automatic snowballs,
too full of magic,
benefit from hairpin turns,
trying to spin around,
walk on water,
and show the world
seeds of carnage.

A lot of misfits
choose to make a gift
of decadent ideas,
banging all night in silence,
defining satellites
as haunted flashlights.

The slow shutter speed of light
looms behind ruined treasure,
Cheop's jazz solo, Dracula's ship,
an alpha dog
found floating in oil.

Flesh-and-blood with grinning mugs,
electrified by oracles
and seasonal monsters,
crawl home from tourist traps
to their isolated pillows.

This was just days before
the happy haze
was shaken by loss.

JOSH HUMPHREY

Whale Songs (Two Villanelles and Eleven Bad Haiku)

> *I would just leave it on, just going again and again and after
> a long while of listening I suddenly realized My God, this thing
> is repeating itself.*
> —Roger Payne

1.
By this time I had called them my only friend
Turning over slowly, spinning in a dance
Tremendous weight made weightless as sand.

I am on a rusted boat. I am on unsure land
And they in their miles unseen, their blue expanse.
By this time I had called them my only friend.

And watched them burst through the surface only to slam
Back into waves every time as if by chance
Tremendous weight made weightless as sand.

From four hundred feet they can see me, just a man
Staring at the constant blue and whitecaps in a trance.
By this time I had called them my only friend

And felt the water that holds their secret with my hands
But it runs through my fingers with just a glance,
Tremendous weight made weightless as sand.

And still they glide through the waves and rest on a strand
Of nothing, an idea of depth, a dark romance.
By this time I had called them my only friend
Tremendous weight made weightless as sand.

2.
By this time I had lost a wife and had a son
In that tiny basement I had made my last bird house.
One way or another all the birds had flown.

And the emergency numbers had abandoned the phone
And the silence always scratching like a mouse.
By this time I had lost a wife and had a son

And slept on the couch heavy as a stone
Half awake with the television in a drowse.
One way or another all the birds had flown.

And the clothes on the stairs like a body thrown
And the bed haphazard—a shoe, a hat, a blouse.
By this time I had lost a wife and had a son

And my hands had forgotten any touch that was known
Far from the shore and the burned-out lighthouse.
One way or another all the birds had flown.

Even when I am here I am never home
This wood and nails, this cold cold house
By this time I had lost a wife and had a son
One way or another all the birds had flown.

3.
But I played those songs
In a room in the dark by myself
And whales sang to me.

And I played those songs
In the silence over and over—
The whales are alive.

And I played those songs
To my mother and my father gone—
The whales in my heart.

And I played those songs
On the ancient wooden intercom—
Whales in my kitchen.

And I took those songs
To men in sunglasses in dark rooms—
Whales on radio.

And I took those songs
To the conductor of New York City—
Whales like a bass drum.

And I took those songs
To the silent nuns in the mountains—
The whales in heaven.

And I took those songs
To the buildings that rise up and rise—
Elevator whale.

And I heard those songs
In a Philadelphia bar—
Whales are everywhere.

And I heard those songs
On the highway on the bridge—
Whales are everywhere.

And I heard those songs
Until they were the whole world over.
The whales and I sleep.

Sestina for the Sahars

We hope to whom we give these tributes is the same one
who holds us in the palm of his hands.
                                    —Paul Emil Sahar

Maurice Maurice please don't be changed. Stay
that beautiful age when you would come to the house
on Livingston, the boys from Fire Island in the kitchen—
the Marios and Alans you called Sweat Pea. Don't change.
Stay with your shirt betraying muscle, face as clear
as sunlight, dancing around to no music at all.

And mysterious brother Christopher we barely saw at all,
just a blur at the birthday dinners and scribbled notes. Stay
that fidgety voice on the telephone, your only clear
language the sound from that piano forgotten in the house,
in whatever corner was closest to your gentle hands. Don't change.
Give your mother those notes to shuffle on in the kitchen—

the smiling heart of that rambling place, the kitchen
with that Arabic candy like concrete fudge and all
the bananas turning black the way you liked, almost changed
to liquid. The big house that she would be the last to stay
in, with all the names to carry, that house
with your lost worn out shoes turned to planters waiting for clear

sky and sun and some Summertime, clean, clear
hose water. The garden wrapping itself around the kitchen
window was the only view of her life, from that house
your father bought new and empty and filled with all
the chairs from Sahar's Upholstery, the leftover ones staying
sometimes for thirty years, their fabric he had changed

himself somehow despite his big mitts and dusty glasses, changed
with those little clove cigarettes dangling, the clear

concentration of his own father, the strength of the center to stay
tight while the edges fray around it, to sit in the kitchen
in that chair he polished with the curve of his body—the king of it all.
And you my friend, my Paul Emil, a specter of that house

even when you were alive, a ghost of that house
in the room that always seemed untouched, spare change
lined up dusty on the dresser, the baseball cards and all
the post-it notes to remind you of our names, to keep it clear
in your mind. Over and over I find myself dumbfounded in my
        kitchen,
thinking of you and wishing you had just lived, just stayed,

stayed to see my house and hold my daughters. It is less and less now I
        wake to dark
and hear you scratching at my kitchen windows, looking and looking.
        But I am changed
forty years on, heart unclear under all it has lost. My old friend, please
        find me.

Sanford

BED

Sanford lies in the only bed for miles
in a house by itself, trees cut to
make walls, logs to hold him up.
The bed is straw and some horse hair
tied up with ropes, so that it sways
with his breathing and this he loves.
It lets him fly in his dreams he tells
his children, over this new land,
the grass and trees so green where
they are tallest and seen from above.
The second river at night calm and

reflecting a sky full of moon.
It is the purpose of it to shine and
the purpose of stars to give light,
our purpose to be in the balance,
the arms of the giants and the Gods.
He will never forget his wife walking
so her steps disturbed nearly nothing,
the soft layers of the world always wet
at heart, the pine, oak and beech leaves,
the bed they will leave as they found it.

SOIL

Sanford sleeps at last in the same soil
that he used to grow the wheat and corn,
rich from the ice age. He will be
surrounded by his line, his sons
who kept him first in mystery and then
in pride, their faces cut up like his own,
like the face of this land he had come
to love as much as his Barbadoes.
He is its child and so sleeps in its embrace.
The birds are his reward, the calls and
songs, the engine of their wings—
pa-chip-chip, gulp-a-pump, ka-ha
cheer-up cheer-up, who-cooks-for-you.
He is warm and cool with seasons
but never cold and gone. The Spring is in
the Winter's sun, sleeping soft and light.

FLOOR

They knocked it down, that old house
and pushed over the gravestones to make
the floor of a garage. They replaced
the ground with stones and then they

---

replaced the stones, replaced the chirping
with the grinding of gears, cut the grass
into tiny boxes and chop it incessantly,
named it all over again for a one-armed
general from the Civil War. Sanford sleeps
deep, undisturbed by motor oil, the fluids
and the cracks. He lies further down still,
the place where nothing is forgot, the earth,
stillness of roots, his land never lost
and at peace. We are left to the concrete,
night cut through with buses and
street lights. The man with the flags
rides his bike up and down up and down
searching for the thing he can't remember.

Another Day in K Town

That same man is drunk-stepping
into the library and he smells
the way I thought and we find
the men's room ceiling full of tiny
vodka bottles again and
the soccer man wants the soccer scores,
but later he will call and ask
three questions about Michael Buble.
The other one is still counting
days sober. He says that when
he gets to one hundred, he is going
to have a drink—just some wine,
nothing major, no biggie.
At least I get to see Polish Joe today
and he has a joke I haven't heard
and the kind of question I can answer.
Today we are in heaven with
this light, the windows from 1907

and the ancient old sun.
It is almost religious the way
Mr. O'Brian folds the newspaper,
every section back in the place
it belongs only today.
Another day, it says, in K Town
or wherever we are, a glory we are here,
we are open eyes and beating hearts.

A Poem for Jason at Last

It was something like you that I wanted to be,
an encyclopedia of bees and a father who literally
left you only paintings of sad clowns in that house
where your mom used the microwave to store bread.

It was something like you that I wanted to be,
coaxing that old truck into movement with
a girl just one Summer shy of art school and
a beard that could claim your face in an afternoon.

I always did regret New Mexico and staying
when I could have gone and never having been
a waiter like I said was my dream and passing
the Summer with my huge Stephen King books.

It was something like you that I wanted to be,
in the Amazon and the castle where they served you
breakfast beer and Cornell University with the
spiral staircases and food that was all muffin delicious.

I stayed to work in the library and keep the stories,
the character in the book no one wants to be.
I stayed on the phone with you into the night and
you would fall asleep and talk from your dream.

It was something like you that I wanted to be.
Who wouldn't want to be the dreamer instead
of the one holding the line? Instead of the life
I wanted, I always dressed for the life I had.

MARK FOGARTY

Dame Edith

*On the night of November 15, 1971, a fashion show at the Santa
Barbara (Calif.) Museum included a segment filmed for the first
reality television show,* An American Family. *Ironically, an icon and
one of the founders of reality on film happened to be there, on the
last night of her life.*

There were cameras at the evening do:
A new type of thing, following people around
Hoping they will rise above the fondue.
There in the corner is an old young woman,
Heiress, socialite, muse, hanging around,
Forgotten dreamgirl now loved by the hour:
Edith Minturn Sedgwick, scion to everything
Bad in the American character from the Mayflower
To the droolings the idle rich plan.

It is the start of something new:
Reality television and the terror of the mundane.
Dame Edith was rarely mundane. This stew
Should have been hers, more than the girls
With the bubble asses or the society girls
Who kept the cameras rolling during sex:
Dame Edith for all her daring was proper, prim,
Mysterious, needy, wondering what's next.
She'd tried her best to escape an American family
And did it as well as any fuckup could.
We fuckups must admire her disdain.
It was her last night on earth, though:
Behind the Music ending grim.
Time to drape a rose on her final flow
Via drugs and booze and questionable sanity.
I dare to think I wouldn't have given her

The downs that ended up killing her,
Would have prodded her to one last
Ride on the chrome horse, one last
Chance to dazzle with her vanity.

She chatted briefly with Lance Loud,
Passing the torch on her last night on earth.
Pity selfies hadn't been invented yet.
All men loved Edie, loved her from birth.
She was lively, pretty, sexy, proud,
With fat raccoon eyes that stab me yet,
A skinny Marilyn. Men tried to capture her
In her leopardskin pillbox hat, in her
Glittering image on a film, in her seedy moonturn
As a goddess in the Chelsea Hotel. I am sorry
It was always capture and release, and release.
Still her life was a triumph not ceasing to cease
Of *catch me if you can while I carry*
My loony lamp brightly, brightest, watch it burn.

Edie had a talent for the ten-second happiness
The rest of us mad ones aspire to, a feel
For the brief caesuras there are to be had,
The gift of gab to document it whole.
The abyss is there all the time, might as well
Skip over it this time, *hey look, there's the empress.*
Yes, she was a waif, yes, her time was gamine.
But Edie made twenty unscripted films
In her seven years in charge of Pharaoh's grain.
She was the queen of reality and its whims,
The American Family for good and bad,
Brilliantly free of it for her time of freefall,
Never a nebbish naked on some isle,
Trotting through the director's taunts,
Her own creation, and you can hold the light:
Do you hear that siren, it's mine,

You haunts have me on loan from the gods,
So take a good look while it shines.
The poets are writing about me tonight,
My glory's like the moon, pale and bright.
America fucked me over, but I won't feel it
If you give me a spike, oh honey boo boo,
There will be time for sadness in a bit
If that's what it comes to, but for now
You'll light my cigarette and wish you knew
My throaty laugh, and how I can plan to debut
The next thing to know about the night.

Songs inspired by Edie Sedgwick:
Femme Fatale (Lou Reed)
Just Like a Woman (Bob Dylan)
Leopardskin Pillbox Hat (Bob Dylan)
Please Crawl Out Your Window (Bob Dylan)
Like a Rolling Stone (Bob Dylan)

Visible Satellites

The *New York Times* didn't have comics,
But anything else you wanted to know was there.
As a kid I pored over the "agate" pages (small type)
To see which ocean liners were docking in New York,
Or where they were going, and a little box
Informed you which satellites were visible in the sky,
And when, and on what course through the heavens.
I looked and looked, and saw Echo 1, Echo 2
Crossing space. I wasn't so far from space!
I could cross the oceans and the oceans of the moon
If I read the *New York Times*.

The cops and the night owls waited for their copies
Of the *Jersey Journal* when the presses cranked at dawn,

Loud as *Cream* with Hendrix sitting in.
The skeins of paper ran along the ceiling,
Black and white birds sailing like kites
Before they would knot together and bang and fall
Onto rollers. I got 50 copies for the newsroom,
And the ink would smear if you touched it.
You can read all day long in a newsroom.
My elbows had patches of ink and I knew more stuff
Than Ken from *Jeopardy*. The pressmen were deaf
And would curse you loudly if you approached.
I stopped the presses many times with mistakes
But never had the nerve to shout it. The deafies
Had no feel for the romance of the presses
Stacked high as Jimi's Marshalls in my memory.

I worked for the sheets for forty years
And never ceased to *kvell* at my name on a page.
I still read the agate pages, which would solemnly report
The results of every rigged wrestling match
(Hogan d. Savage, Madison Square Garden, World Wrestling
          Federation)
As well as the track reports from St. Benedict's,
And Pogo's latest musings, and the "woman's" page
With its legendary (probably mythic) headline
For debutantes this year it's balls, balls, balls.
I had instructions from five editors
To bring them Royko's column the minute
It moved on the wires, when I wasn't trying to puzzle out
The blurry words on the newly invented fax machine,
Or how the purple ink from UPI got carried to my underwear.

There's a dock somewhere where I can still
Board those solemn liners in the inky night.

I wonder if Echo I and II still loop the world in flight?
My elbows aren't black any more; I guess that's a good thing.

The prints are slowly stopping their presses
Except when the newsreaders say, "Breaking news
From the *Washington Post*! This just in
From the *New York Times*!"

The red stuff was fake at those wrestling matches,
But the sheets can still bloody the nose of a President.

*Echo 1 was originally loosely estimated to survive until soon after its fourth
dip into the atmosphere in July 1963, but it ended up living much longer than
these estimates and reentered Earth's atmosphere, burning up on May 24,
1968 (Wikipedia).*

What I'd Say to Columbus

She told me she was from Puerto Rico.
Something when she turned her face made me say,
"Are you Indian? Taino?"

She startled, and flushed. "How did you know?
My father called me his little Taina."

I know a few things.
I know Christopher Columbus was great and terrible.
Great at sailing; terrible, odious running the show.
I have no Taino, but I know enough that if I saw his toxic ships
Pull up again off the coast of Puerto Rico I'd say,
"You made a wrong turn, dude. It's south
To the Indies, around the Cape of Good Hope,
Now *that's* a transit that will rattle your bones.
Don't let the door hit you in the ass!"

My Taina was there to learn to finance homes for Indians.
I wish I remembered her better.

Was her dark hair like a waterfall? I don't think so.
Well, maybe like the kind that flows inside homes,
That nourish the soul of a place to live.
Were her lips like Pantone Red? I can't remember
If they were. I'm sure they were a perfect color
The many times she said she had the money
For a place to establish your house, your treasure.

I have spent a few nights in Puerto Rico,
Once in a forest where the birds never slept,
Where I left the glass door open as they whistled all night long,
Nourished by vivid seeds that would defy any empire.

It's a sin to kill a mockingbird for they sing so sweetly.

My Taina turned to apply herself
To the less-than-vivid rules that apply
To mortgage finance in Florida.
I wish I remembered her better.
She is my treasure, my transit, my hearth.

I remember now the sharp, wonderful bones of her cheeks
When she turned to navigate the HUD 184.
I remember her now. She'll do
For a statue.

Though the Taino tribe died out due to Western contact, many in the Greater Antilles retain substantial Taino DNA. In 2010, 10,000 people identified themselves as Taino in Puerto Rico.

Where People Go When They Die

I'd been thinking in that valley
of dreams and half dreams, that place between

states neither awake nor dreaming,
of my parents, aunts and uncles,
how they left one right after another,
as if they'd heard a call to come home,
called in by a voice they longed to hear.

Someone wanted to shake my hand.
I reached out but they took their hand away.
Instead, hand after hand reached for mine,
took it from above with shadowy fingers
from where they must live somehow
in a new valley between shadows and dreams,
in a new and empathetic homeland.

Irish translation by JOHN L. FOGARTY

An áit a imíonn daoine tar éis bás.

Bhí mé ag smaoineamh san ailt sin
Bruadar 'is leath-bhruadar, an áit sin idir
Cruthanna ní múscailte ní bringlóideach,
de mo thuismitheoirí, aintíní, 'is uncailí,
an chaoi a d'fhág siad duine i ndiadh an duine,
mar chuala siad glaoch orthu a teacht abhaile,
glaoite isteach le glór a mba mhian leo a cloisteáil.

Ba mhian le duine mo lámh a chroitheadh,
Shín amach mé ach rug siad a lámh uaim.
Ina áit sin, shín amach lámh i ndiadh lámh,
Ag breith greim orm anuas le méara síofrúla
As an áit a chaithfidh siad ina gcónaí ar chaoi éigin
I ngleann nua idir scáthanna 'is bruadair
I dtír dhúcais nua 'is ceanúil ar fad.

Literal Translation: This is bad English, but it will give you an idea of the way the Irish express themselves.

An áit a imíonn daoine tar éis bás.
The place that people go off to after death

Bhí mé ag smaoineamh san ailt sin
I was [at] thinking in that deep-sided glen [there is no pluperfect in Irish]
Bruadar 'is leath-bhruadar, an áit sin idir
Of dreams and half-dreams, that place between
Cruthanna ní múscailte ní bringlóideach,
States neither awake nor dreamlike,
De mo thuismitheoirí, aintíní, 'is uncailí,
of my parents, aunts and uncles,
An chaoi a d'fhág siad duine i ndiadh an duine,
the way that they left a person[one] following a person [another]
mar chuala siad glaoch orthu a teacht abhaile,
As if they heard a call upon them to come home,
glaoite isteach le glór a mba mhian leo a cloisteáil.
Called out by a voice that would be a wish for them to hear.

Ba mhian le duine mo lámh a chroitheadh,
Was a wish by someone my hand to shake,
Shín amach mé ach rug sé a lámh uaim.
I reached out, but he took his hand from me.
Ina áit sin, shín amach lámh i ndiadh lámh,
In its place, reached out hand after hand,
Ag breith greim orm anuas le méara síofrúla
Grasping upon me from above with elfin fingers
As an áit a chaithfidh siad ina gcónaí ar chaoi éigin
From a place that they must be in their living in some way
I ngleann nua idir scáthanna 'is bruadair,
In a new valley between shadows and dreams
I dtír dhúcais nua 'is ceanúil ar fad.
In a native land new and quite loving, affectionate.

—Murchadh Ó Fógartaigh

This is the old name: sea-warrior; Marcus is used in Irish but it came in with the Normans. Brian Boru's 'crown prince' at Clontarf was Murchadh mac Briain.

SUSANNA LEE

Unspoiled

That doe, living in the woods behind my house, teaches her children:
how to lie perfectly still until she returns to nurse them;
how quick one must leap at the smell of wolf,
and how to trust one's instinct to find the right direction to run away;
how to nudge aside the snow with the snout,
to nibble at the promise of moss beneath;
to believe that when the moss runs out,
the barren trees
will sustain life;
how to eat bark in the dead of winter,
and how long one must chew
before swallowing;
to trust in Nature,
to remain unspoiled.

I, too, am unspoiled, yet no wiser than the doe.

Her eldest,
this deer, lying on the far side of the road;
now mangled, twitching, splayed limbs akimbo;
gashes in his throat spewing, gushing red;
now stilling;
knew nothing of the factory wherein those headlights were
        manufactured.

I, too, am unspoiled, and no wiser than the doe.
I do not read what's been written.
I say,
the view from atop the shoulders of giants
is directly above the spot where, once, they had decided it was the
        perfect place to firmly plant their feet.
They've now been rooted for thousands of years.

Those who've read all of what's been written take this treasure trove
        seriously
and attempt to sequester it in an ark floating in gray matter.

However, that boat's already leaking:
favorite recipes for chocolate chip cookies,
manuals for repairing Mac trucks,
guidebooks for traveling the Appalachian Trail,
poems sensing there are frays along the hems of bell-bottomed
        blue jeans;
all, stories we tell ourselves, over and over.

The better and better wars they, the learned, convince one another
        to create
are simply the bubbling over,
so much scum hovering atop the floating bits of ham in split pea soup.

I'm unlearned, fresh, unspoiled;
hoping to remain outside the box and discover why boxes are blinding.

I refuse to cede my innocent wholeness.
Like the doe, I retain the ideas I was born with,
those that sustained my forbears
when even the potatoes wouldn't maintain their integrity.

In my poems, I do not make reference to ancient Greeks,
whose wisdom is said to be as yet unsurpassed.
I don't read them.
I do not deny them their experiences. I take their word for it.
Or, rather, the word of those who've read them, studied them, recited
        by rote their verse,
then inevitably anguished over those ancient explorers' deep voyages
        into meaning.

I do adore writers who cannot write an English line
without discovering the patterns of the shadows of Icarus's wings
darkening their pages.
I enjoy imagining their privileged lives,
seeing how their curiosity led them to prowl through crumbling
        intellectual ruins.
I delight in finding evidence that dwelling on past writings
        has eviscerated their hearts.

I, on the other hand, will explore literary scholarship no further.
Unacquainted with history, science, mind-travelers, I'm untainted.
I cherish my own guile.

I will persevere.
I'll never give up.
I will seek and discover the reason why
only the tears of dolphins and not elephants heal unicorns.

I will learn
how to move each of my own atoms independently of the others,
using nothing but the force of gluons.

Yes, and I will spend my free time in knitting,
out of the resounding echoes of the midnight howls of just seven
        coyotes,
enough joy and peace to blanket all the world.

This deer, lying on the far side of the road;
now mangled, twitching, splayed limbs akimbo;
gashes in her throat spewing, gushing red;
now stilling;
knew nothing of the factory wherein those headlights
        were manufactured.

Three Poems for My Father

I. My Dad Might Die Today

My dad is drinking no water.
They are keeping him "comfortable."
My dad might die today.

I plan his obituary.

I wish
I had paid more attention
when he explained to me
how to fix a Delta faucet.

II. The Day

The day my father died
hasn't happened yet.

The horses walk along this fence
at sunset.
What is their destination?

Are they hospice horses,
trained to entertain
those waiting at death's door,
who might want more?

If I open these French doors,
will anyone notice?

Could I catch a beautiful horse
and ride it over the hill
into the sunset?

III. Sailing

Sailing
    a boat on water
        is easy.

Turning
    a hospital room . . . into a cove,
    and a hospital bed . . . into a yacht,
    and a push-button call device . . . into a captain's wheel
        takes some navigation.

Pebble

That summer day,
I hung upside-down
from the limb over the pond in Heater's field.

I threw in the last pebble
of the handful I had swiped from your top dresser drawer.

I needed to see,
not the splash,
but concentric circles.

I needed to feel the pale of predictable.
I had to find the steel of even.
I all but imploded, desiring an anti-chaos.

The pebble dropped slowly, unwillingly, from my open palm.
It sat on the surface of the water for a full two seconds,
then slipped through and disappeared below.

It came right back up,
leapt a foot into the air,

and stopped,
hovering above,
within the arc of the pond's breath.

The pebble was dry.

I could hear its soft rasping,
like the shifting whisper of a damselfly,
asking forgiveness for breaking the tension,
for riling the stillness of the waters.

Locust

I am locust.
Fear my jaws, my crunching song,
God's call to reap what you sow.

God's great abundance is not a mistake.
Sow what you'll need.
Cede first fruits to priests,
then feed the good food to the mighty.
Gather the rest and eat your fill.

Are some grains less than perfect?
Allow the least to glean.
Seek those willing to get down on hands and knees
and pick the stalks clean.

Starve me, hated locust.
Leave nothing in the field, or my numbers will soar.
I'll return with a vengeance year after year
with ravenous appetite.

I'll darken your skies in an instant,
come to feast on memories,

unappreciated past harvests.

You'll hear my horde hum
just beyond the horizon.

The approaching jaws of the tiny,
in terrifying numbers,
tot up your sins.

The deafening chomp wakes you to reason.
You've created your own destruction.

I descend in season so you shall know
you reap what you sow.

I am locust, servant to God,
His chosen vengeance
for man's greed, selfishness, and sloth.

Camping for One

This year, I'll be alone with the crickets
under the rising moon of my misery.
I'll mourn outside my empty tent,
pretending, as I did when I was single,
my silver flute is a steel-stringed guitar.
In my best Joan Baez,
I'll croon cowboy songs and nursery rhymes
and tunes of sad and happy times.
In evening's cicadas and midnight's owls,
I'll hear echoes of the past.
I'll fear spiders and snakes.
Raccoons might take to rustling under my tent.
I'll make peace with a hint of bears,
and enjoy the setting sun.

BILL MORELAND

While Waiting at the 165 Local Bus Stop

Angelo's eyes are set wide apart,
his oily hair is bed-headed,
matted down, brown.

He wore a black knitted scarf
with thick wool links loosely woven,
wrapped around,
and around,
halfway up his head.

His speech bursts in rapid fire,
high-pitched
puppy yelps
(that scarf snagged a spit ball gob
like a foul ball stuck
in the links
of the backstop fence).

Breathing through snot-packed nostrils
came Angelo lumbering,
labored,
and carting with him a large canvas painting called

Gloria on the Rocks.

She was beautiful.

He told us he had worked on this painting for eight months.
It was a thick acrylic
packed with electric blue sea waves
that crashed silently,
moisture-less

upon the pedestal—
her rock.

From the bottom to the top
the blue hues darkened to navy
flecked with speckles
way off in the distance,
straight on
in to
Heaven.

Gloria was his mom's name.

She stood in a long sleeveless red red gown,
her dirty blonde curls gently waving down
and across her shoulders.
Her arms were outstretched,
beckoning,
her palms turned upwards,
beseeching.

Ah, Gloria!

Behind her,
adding a touch of extra-medium,
Angelo glued on real feathers for wings.

He used to get picked on in school a lot.
He drooled and doodled mostly,
got an F for "embarrassing the History teacher,"
and, for embarrassing him,
Angelo broke his Social Studies teacher's nose,
but knows now that
that was wrong.

And so, he loves his art,

his therapy.

He's first on that bus,
we all followed behind.
In excited, unstoppable chatter,
Angelo gathered his canvas and bags;
flustered,
he clattered to his usual seat.

He told us he's giving this painting to a friend
that is blind,
and hopes to describe it well.

Angelo will.

Industrial Parts

    1.   The Man

Josef's haircut was a fury brown burr.
With a red, greasy rag, he wiped the plump, shaved, baby porcupine
that is his fat neck.
Muscle memory slapped the levers of the lathe,
adjusted his chuck,
tugged his nuts inside his briefs,
and transformed metal razor shavings into
a spiraling bundle of steel wool
that dropped around his oil-soaked
Sears and Roebuck
steel-toe boots.

In the foundry trays there are, bathed
in the thick sickening sweetness of oil,
tiny precision parts, funneling
somewhere to assemble themselves into some whole completed

something.

The cutting tool's blue-hot chamfered tip held steady.
Twenty times for every one 'mississippi',
speeding alloy metal bits turned,
and cut, threaded to tolerances of
one ten-thousandth of an inch.
Twelve rapid-fire machines
punched out eighty-six-thousand-four-hundred screws,
per shift,
for armaments
or precision surgical instruments.

The machinist serves both ends of the bullet.

In broken English, that Kraut cursed the Filipino kid on the hi-lo:

*Pineapple! Haul your ass and put doze castings on der pallet dere,
shtoopid.*

Through his reach, feeding his machines,
motion and commotion,
Josef conducted a metal-on-metal
cutting choir
which sang,

Oy yea Oy yea Oy yea,

and from it
arced yellow sparks,
trailing blue smoke
comet flagellum
which either singed pockmarks on his face, stinging,
or they evaporated altogether.

The operator and the operation:

there is magnificence in this ugliness,
and each
has a casual audacity.

2. The Method

Near Newark Sewage, I was parked in Delawanna's parking lot; they
render fat. My windows were down; it was hot. I heard what sounded
like a large bee hive; it was not. They were flies. Teed up on a flatbed
truck, one dozen fifty-five gallon drums were on deck; each one open
with pig carcasses, haunches and heads, stuck out. Foreman flies
hovered. Worker maggots scoured. A colony of iridescent wings and
blue-green bodies shimmied in the sun; the swirling efficacy licked
clean the cavities of the beasts' hollowed-out eyes. *They* were the
unannounced sub-contractors; their pre-rendering was startling,
prepping, as they did, this primary ingredient for soap.

3. The Machine

And over time,
with stone, or bronze, or steel,
in clumsy chunks,
have we stacked
false starts
to act civilized.

Through trial and error,
upon shifting layers
of failures,
come new successes,
planned obsolescences,
quickly succumbed
by improvement.

Cinder fingers
write in the dust.

Sorrowful singers
cry at the dusk.

Diligent dilettantes
carry the musk.

Maniacal militants
march over rust.

A pattern of pillage,
of plunder, of rubble.

Towering baubles,
the dunces will babble

ker-plunking

still lower

into the grave

we'll grovel,

till those

saints

do call

us

home.

Oy yea Oy yea Oy yea.

Recycling Day

I'm sitting on a cheap and shallow concrete balcony
hazed in L.A.
The clouds of Wu Tang, poontang and the Marlboro Man
linger.
The fast food fans billow both garlic
and the Spanish cusses of the dishwashers
bent over their sinks,
thinking out loud.

Dumpsters and kitty cats
caked in ketchup
knock and rock
BEEP BEEP BEEP
while the garbage truck is singing its back up song.

And I'm thinking of you.

Like spiders
crawling across chicken scratch
my thoughts
I'm writing on the back
of a health card cancellation
notification.

I see bogus treasure in your sunken eyes.
Beneath your wrinkled dugs a lead anvil lies.
The truth rings in the hammer beats
bound in chains and counterfeit love,
both forged.

My ashtray, my drinks, your love
. . . all smoked.

If the sun were out, I wouldn't know it.
If the sky were black how could I show it
to that dark star you call a heart?

I don't expect much, but I demand it all!

Sonogram

He doesn't want you and I need him.

Bye-Bye Baby Bye-Bye

I can't do this again.

Bye-Bye Baby Bye-Bye

I'm too young to do this.

Bye-Bye Baby Bye-Bye

I'm too old to do this.

Bye-Bye Baby Bye-Bye

I can't do this alone.

Bye-Bye Baby Bye-Bye

You were conceived in violence!

Bye-Bye Baby Bye-Bye

My Pappy's your Pappy.

Bye-Bye Baby Bye-Bye

I cannot care for
Or afford you.

Bye-Bye Baby Bye-Bye

I'm expecting the unexpected.

Bye-Bye Baby Bye-Bye

It's a life change I can't deal with.

Bye-Bye Baby Bye-Bye
There are too many among us.

Bye-Bye Baby Bye-Bye

It's your birthday next week,
You're the gift that God gave me.
My gift is one day
Take a look, one last breath
And let God
Take you away.

Bye-Bye Baby Bye-Bye

It's either you or it's me

Bye-Bye Baby Bye-Bye

I want you and can't keep you,

Bye-Bye Baby Bye-Bye

To hold you inside me,

Bye-Bye Baby Bye-Bye

But never beside me.

Bye-Bye Baby Bye-Bye

My choices are hard won,
My choices are hard ones.
Hard choices,
You among them.
Free choice is my voice.
My voice is to choose,
And to choose is to lose.
Still it's mine
All mine,
Alone.

Bye-Bye Baby Bye-Bye
Boom Boom Boom Boom Boom Boomp
Boom Boom Boom Boom Boom Boomp   Boom Boompff

CLAUDIA SEREA

Cold

It was so cold,
the war had frozen over.

I could see my breath in the classroom,
fluffy like cotton yarn,
and my teacher's,
and my high school colleagues'.

At home, I'd place my hands
over the reading lamp
to turn them from blue
to red.

Mom bought fabrics, lining, batting, and snaps,
and made my brother and me ski costumes
to wear to school.

We slept with wool hats,
wool socks, wool mittens,
and wool sweaters so thick
they were bullet- and moth-proof.

My breath turned to dew on the wall,
then froze into intricate flowers
and vines.

It was so cold,
the actors on the stage had visible breath,
and the theatre audience
breathed in Shakespeare's verse
and exhaled cirrus wisps.

The bride and groom kissed non-stop
to keep warm,
and the wedding guests spoke white words
before the food arrived.

It was so cold,
the rocks cracked open.

The doctors breathed white gauze
as if ghosts were present
in the operating rooms
before opening
the patients' steaming bellies.

It was so cold,
my circus lady neighbor
brought home the pythons
so they wouldn't freeze,
and kept them in the bathtub.

She wore them to work,
a tight suit
under her mink fur.

For decades, it was cold, cold.

Each one of us exhaled
a small cloud,

proof we were alive.

Arsonist August

The car is a flea,

moving through the vast brown fur
of the plain.

The sky is closer here,
and drips on the molten asphalt.

We drive through scorched fields
of sunflowers with heads bowed,
accepting death,

and through towns full of beggars
and kids with stray dog eyes.

Inside the churches, Jesus watches
from a safe distance.

Burnt concrete walls
with black graffiti:
"As punishment,
they grant our wishes."

But the countryside is ruled by zinnias,
in Romanian *cârciumãrese*—
women pub keepers.

From church to pub to cemetery,
a simple trajectory.

Clopping slowly,
the cows come home,
swaying their hips
like clumsy heavy ladies
in high heels.

We drive over hills,
over the smoldering hills

and through the charred
gilded corn.

We drive under the storks' wedding
rotating in the sky,
a clock telling us it's time.

Ahead of us,
August sets fire to more fields.

The road home belongs
to those who dare.

Baby teeth

I return to you, dirt road,
keeper of all truths.

Let me take off my socks
to feel the softness
of your dust.

Grandmother's house was never sold—
it was left to crumble.

One sleeping room
with two beds
with straw mattresses

and the kitchen
with no fridge
and a two-eyed
electric range.

I remember the whitewashed walls
made of clay and chaff,

and the thatch roof
over which my brother and I used to throw
our baby teeth
for good luck.

Thick moss was on the roof.

Now there must be branches
and twigs pushing through
the caved-in walls.

At night, the moon still searches

for our baby teeth
through all the dark crevices.

Linden flower tea

We spread them out to dry
on the kitchen table,
on newspapers,
over the photos of the beloved leader.

The fragrance lit the rooms.

Tilia, the lime, or linden trees—
from Middle English *lind,*
Latin *lentus*, "flexible,"
and German *lind*, "lenient, yielding"—

stretched for centuries
their shade across empires,
lining their avenues.

We drank a lot of linden flower tea,
the Prozac of the past,
said to relieve insomnia, anxiety,
get rid of migraines,
depression, fever, flu,
and wrinkles.

For us, it was breakfast.

In winter, Mom made the infusion
in a blue tin pot,
and we had tea each morning
with a slice of bread
and marmalade.

The tea was the only gift of the streets,
a mild, sweet-scented sedative,

feeble attempt to conjure summer
from honey, steam,
and petals ground to dust.

It's almost time to pick the linden blooms.

I hear they are sold by the bagfuls
by Gypsies at every subway entrance
in Bucharest.

No one here picks them.

No one drinks
linden flower tea,

or thinks the golden pollen is romantic,
or even useful.

No one, but the bees.

I hear them
in the intoxicating canopy
on Wood Street.

You won't know this love

You won't know this love
until you'll know each mole,
each constellation
on her skin

until you'll recognize her skin scent
and crave it at night.

You'll feel the need to touch,
to carry
your little monkey
on your back.

The urge of milk,
eyes closed,

the urge to pull the zippers tight,
to cover, to protect.

You won't know this love
until you'll feel your rib
missing her rib,

the ocean of your blood
seeking her ship.

ZORIDA MOHAMMED

It Was Her Legs That Bore the Brunt

She was never vain about her body.
Midwives Emily, and her sister Gertrude,
coaxed 11 of us out of her.
She always preferred Emily.

When it was my turn to wash her for the first time,
her embarrassment came out as irritability.
She was helpless and shut her eyes
as I parted the petals of her dark, velvety,
rose-like flower. There were no scars, no striations,
no baby making marks that I was expecting to see.
It was her legs that showed the scars;
it was her legs that bore the brunt of the burdens she bore
in her early married life, caring for my grandparents,
raising us kids, raising goats and chickens,
tending the garden, toting water
from the village stand pipe.

With each stroke of the wash cloth
I talked baby talk to her the way she did
when she tended us kids.
I had to tell her, "*wot a pretty poonie.*"
Her body had fallen apart on the inside.
Her skin was fragile and transparent,
and made it nearly impossible to lift or move her,
but her *sugar-cake,* her *garlic,* her *poonie*
remained intact and enviable.

When medicine blew up her breasts
way past Dolly Parton's,
she bought oversized bras,
and *I* got angry for her.

I don't know where her rage of yore went
when she tried to knead me into the ground
with her knees and fist,
my hair in one fist for leverage,
as she heaped on her helplessness.

      *   *   *

She became a woman I did not recognize in her later years.
I'd gone from shameless, lazy, dotish, a George Street whore
(because of my raucous laughter)
to someone she revered, deferred to.
Some of my sibs took notice,
grew burrs in their craw.

I'd come to America to help them
out of the little Kolkota
they'd dug themselves into in El Dorado,
she and father brooding eleven,
my grandfather and grandmother's ambition
never rising above the dirt floor
and mango trees in their yard.

I came to America because of my father,
a tireless plough horse
who was generous with his car-fixing and engineering skills
to anyone in our prejudiced village.

I came to America before I knew he had heart disease
and would die of it, like his mother and father,
the two people who made indelible marks on me.

I emulated my grandfather but did not become a rake.
I became addicted to words on paper
and hounded anything in print.

I learned how not to be

---

from my playmate grandmother
who whispered about everybody,
and cursed the breeze if it blew on her
the wrong way.

"She Gone Through"

She'd been going through even before I met her.

On 2nd Sunday, Tanty Dolly hid in the latrine
when her husband came for her.
She'd escaped the fearsome-looking man
of her arranged marriage,
and stepped blindly into bliss with Pandoo,
her brother-in-law's brother,
the curly-haired crooner
who made Indians born in Trinidad
lilting weak with longing for India,
a place they'd never been.

Pandoo took her to his little *juppa*
in the bush someplace behind God's back.

They ate *lappe* and *gootie,*
wild meat he hunted in the forest.

The only shine in the place
was from human wear,
footsteps that had polished
the sloping entrance into the dark space
they called home.

But she lived next to a field of *katchoo* lilies,
lush white lilies just outside her door.

When I visited, we picked the lilies
and boiled the bitter out.
She curried them with slices of green mango
into a tangy country dish.

Between crop season and rum—
the elixir he could not live without—
hunger drove her from Pandoo.

He knew how to beg and promise.
She vowed she'd never return to him.

She hid in a friend's house.
He found her and begged and promised.
His tears fell on the porch in the dark.
Then there was a chest-tightening thud.

They found him and an empty bottle,
the drink foaming from his mouth.

She squatted with her children
in a new place in the bush.
Bit by bit, they raised a roof
and added nice doors.

The government ran a road in her front yard.
Her "eyeball," her favorite son,
was shot in a mistaken identity.

A nursing home was no place on Xmas day.
Her son brought her to see her favorite sister.
She lay in the back seat unable to sit up.
When the car pulled away,
"She gone through"
was all my mother could say.

Kiskee Morning and Dog Chorus Night

Trinidad is nothing as I left it, not even the Northern Range,
yet it is more of itself than I could ever dream.
Even the misguided lane meanders
into the right stream.

Concrete, concrete, concrete everywhere,
the sidewalk, the street, the houses.
Concrete walls growing
where there were once hibiscus or sweet olive fences.
The gravel hill leading into the gutter is now paved over.

Mrs. Jordan's old English garden is a slab of concrete.
Her old ixoras, oleanders and jasmine replaced
by palms and other vocal tropical splash in pots.
Her mango, calabash and cashew trees
are replaced by a clean sweep of concrete.

A thick carpet of dried leaves
alerted her to visitors.

A dog barks somewhere in the gutter,
and, one by one, all the village dogs
are barking, up and down the hill,
each dog catching on, ignited
like a bit of oxygen on a few stray straws
in a wild fire that doubles back on itself
in a cul de sac
until it tires out,
extinguishing itself.

Ganesh's Flowers

Vayu, the God of wind
has blown a few of Ganesh's flowers
out of the lingam-shaped dome
that shelters him
near the main door of the Hindu school.

To gain Ganesh's favor,
devout Hindu students snip
flowers along the way to school.
Those who are jolted into consciousness

---

at the sight of Ganesh, waiting at the door,
scramble to pluck any flower within reach.
They thrust their hands through the wrought iron fence
of my mother's yard, across from the school,
in a last ditch effort at appeasement.

New beginnings, removal of obstacles
and facilitator of learning
are some of Ganesh's specialties.

I have a mind to tell the flower-nappers
that Ganesh does not accept stolen flowers,
and create a mean consternation
to save the flowers.

Always in My Heart

As we drive along in our enigmatic moment,
you turn the radio on
and, in the middle of a lilting instrumental number,
you ask me to name the tune.

When did you get so "creolized," father?
Where did you get your western ear,
growing up in our little Indian village
playing beesh all day with the sardines in the river
until dusk sets you on the path to your mother
who will chase you,
until she catches a glimpse
of the bamboo knot behind your back
packed with sardines?
Into her happy hands it goes,
lulling her into frying them for supper.

So this is what you do
when you leave us to drive your taxi,

your fine red and white taxi!
Picking up strangers all night
and listening with them
to western tunes,
becoming like them,
until you are tired
and return to us
asleep in our little dirt house,
the lively mantle of music slipping off
somewhere along the way home.

The car stops,
and I'm getting out.
You are smiling at me.
"Always In My Heart."
My father is talking about his heart!
He sees that I am flustered:
"The tune: it's called "Always In My Heart."

My feet meet the pavement, and I shut the door.
I am reaching for my sister's hand
as you drive off to look for passengers
and play your radio politely
as you take them to their destinations.

JOHN BARRALE

The Essex Street Market

When I was little, my grandfather and I went there
just before Easter
to buy a lamb's head.

The lambs were tethered in open pens.

When you passed, they tugged at their ropes
and looked at you with bloodshot eyes.
Saliva dripped from their muzzles.

Butchers' helpers, boys not much older than me,
poured buckets of water on the cutting tables
to clean them.

Watery blood puddled on the straw
under the tables.

Mounds of lungs still slippery with life
and stacks of fat hearts and thick tongues
were also sold.

Everything was by weight.

The eyes of the heads seemed to look at you
when they were lifted from their bed of ice
and onto the scale's shiny steel pan.

The eyes gave me nightmares.

Expanses of dirty glass crisscrossed the ceiling
and let the light in.

On a sunny day, the light was pink.

* * * * *

My grandfather always held my hand
when we walked home.

If I could paint, my fingers,
twined in his,
would be muted,

the tapping of his cane
a color
as cold and quiet
as stone.

The soul fades until it is gone.
If we are lucky, someone
remembers the colors.

When my brother died,
my fingertips
traced his face
and closed his blue,
staring eyes.

I only saw my grandfather in his coffin.
His eyes were closed.

In life, I remember they were brown.

I was always afraid
and never tasted the heads
my grandfather bought.

Milked-over, from the heat

of the oven, their eyes
were gray.

Childhood

It's hard to believe how normal it was
to live in small rooms.

I shared a bedroom
with my two brothers.

I was lucky. The eldest.
My bed touched the wall.
I slept alone. Sal and Richard
shared the room's other bed.

My father was orderly. Old army.
So everything was kept neat.

My mother was the kingdom's queen.
I remember clouds and pastures
in the fabric on her bed.

You could see treetops in smudges
from her bedroom window.

She always said we would visit
 a magic lake
where she sang a song
when she was young.

We never did.

September, 1964—when they played "The House of the Rising Sun"

Though I don't remember the color of her eyes, when we were
      together
the moon rose in its gun, and time was put on hold like a chambered
      shell.
Our bodies were hot-wired, came together, the lines blurred, a smear
of light and speed, the crooked little stars falling like her yes and no.
This I remember: the wind like a thrown knife under the bridge,
the snap of gum in her mouth, the far-off gull sound of her sigh
when she let me slip my hand under her bra.

She knew me well, understood the music was my devil.
She saw the marks of hesitation, found my seams and ripped.
Was she beauty or religion,
or just that song
when I turned fifteen?

Her Cat in the Window Blue with Rain

I remember
her cat
in the window
blue
with rain,

and slow April mornings,

the pages
of her
favorite books
turning
on the table,

breakfast scant

like her robe
printed
with flowers,

the taste of cigarettes,
and black coffee
sharp,

the sugar brown
and stirred in
with a white
plastic spoon.

I remember
her legs
dangling
over the edge
of the bed,

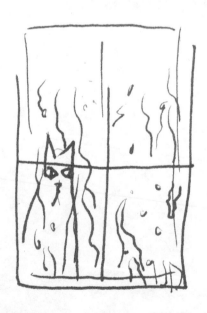

and the small
whisker sound
of nylons
pulled off
and on,

and the shyness
when she showed me
the broken china
she collected
and kept
in a box.

I remember
making love
on her
November-colored
rug,

her lace
and oyster
taste,

and the moon
coming through
the window

with its light

pale

on her belly.

I remember
Rue St. Denis
in December

covered in ice
and snow,

and the café
like a shiny miracle

open

at the bottom
of the hill,

the thin stems
of the wine glasses
twirling,

the bottles of wine
lined up in rows
so formal
and French.

I remember
her happy face
sitting across from me

and the bowl
of onion soup
we shared,

she closing
around
her pleasure
like the petals
of a flower,

she simple,
and there,

her face like her life,
creased with dreams.

Turiddu, the Viking

—for my grandfather

Ships with billowing sails
and masts like crosses
filled his stories.

He in the telling
again in lost places

where narwhales
and giant sea turtles
swam,

and where the bleat
of terns and gulls
filled the air

over floating mountains
of ice,

and where, one fearsome night,
the moon rose
like a golden horse

as he watched the lowering
of the long boats.

Sent to hunt the whale, they were,
he said,

twelve strong men pulling
at the oars

while he, a boy,
and a cook's helper,
shivered
on the windy, frozen deck.

All these things he said he saw.

A world, perhaps,
that never was.

Or, simply now, was hidden
behind his tired eyes.
My brother and I were his beloved,
his boats bobbing in the ocean
of his blood.

Come the distance, you did,
he once said.

And with a nod,
or a gesture with his pipe,
his ringed fingers pointing
like a jeweled sexton,
he'd set our course out on the sea
and among the stars,
his simple words
erasing the dirty dusk
and mean streets.

And yes, like his picture,
he was handsome,
even then when old.

And yes, he was a sailor,
fancied himself a Viking
from old Scandia stock.

No one believed him.
Not even me.

ANTON YAKOVLEV

No Place for Horseshoes

I

I'm stuck in a field by the river, trying to make sense
of all the logs piled up on the shore.
The river is so narrow, it just isn't serious.
And someone has planted carrots nearby.
He has walked over a narrow log to cross it,
and now splinters are floating below.
The current of the river is counterbalanced
by the wind: the splinters stand still.

Back in the hut, a boy had compared himself
to a wooden peg in the wheels of love.
I was one with every wooden peg in the world,
but I didn't know it.

II

Eight years later, doctors with scalpels
are patrolling my house. So lazy they've grown,
they didn't even bother to wash the blood off.
And a sarcastic girl, a good friend of mine,
is recounting with a grin her experience
with throwing laboratory rats against the wall.
She must have killed thousands in this manner
and will undoubtedly kill thousands more.
Pegs in the wheel.
                    Medieval torture devices
have ceded their place to sophisticated torture devices.
In a barn beyond their sight, my harp lies broken.
At dawn, my head floats gently down the river.

The Forgotten Years

Slammed a wall in halo creation process
Packed a holy twister into a postcard
Rags are lifted from cooling corpses
Hoping for a chance encounter, but the churches

Packed a holy twister into a postcard
On a night of rarely worn sunglasses
Hoping for a chance encounter, but the churches
Converge to view a punctuated flashback

On a night of rarely worn sunglasses
Human bodies expand, twelve hours later
Converge to view a punctuated flashback
Unambiguously marked on a wooden pole

Human bodies expand, twelve hours later
Faces become mountains through the window
Unambiguously marked on a wooden pole
In your garden that turned to silence

Faces become mountains through the window
Fallen out of syntax, music lost color
In your garden that turned to silence
Lit by hummingbirds. Breathing

Fallen out of syntax, music lost color
Slammed a wall in halo creation process
Lit by hummingbirds. Breathing
Rags are lifted from cooling corpses

The Windows Above

Trying not to snore, the illegal immigrant
falls asleep on the street. He dreams
of some heavily strutting citizens in the windows above
who spend their days taking smoky semi-nude pictures.

He decides to do some visual work himself
and installs a hidden camera in their home,
burning DVDs of their strutting
and slipping them under their door every week or so.

The citizens freak, and for a while they really don't know
what to do, until they're stricken by the idea
to dress up as the Pope for all of their future strutting.
Wearing Pope's costumes, they find peace of mind again
and do many more photo shoots.

—

A rapper uses a 17-year-old prostitute
and feels secretly guilty about it.
He doesn't tell his buddies about his feelings,
claims he's not taking any of this too seriously.
The 17-year-old is a trust fund baby
and is just trying to live outside of her comfort zone.

One day the rapper shows up and starts yelling at her,
pretending she's his girlfriend and they're breaking up.
She glares at him. That makes him so ashamed of himself,
he hides in the closet, where he just happens to find
a Pope's costume she wore some past Halloween.

He puts on the costume and feels much better.
He comes back out of the closet, seduces her,
pays her more than her going rate and waltzes away.

So far as I know, he still uses her services,
always wearing her Pope's costume during their rendezvous.

—

One day, an ace pilot drags out his old private airplane
and trucks it to an intersection not far from where
the immigrant sleeps and the prostitute does her laundry.
He tries to fly the plane vertically, with almost no running start.
When he takes off, the pilot sees his own hometown
in a way he has never seen it before:

every tile on the roof of this red-roofed neighborhood
looks like a Pope's costume, *is* a Pope's costume.
In every window, lovers kiss in Pope's costumes.
Wanderers walk their Westies, dressed in Westie Pope's costumes.
The pilot is so distracted, he loses control of the airplane,
which looks like a Pope's costume in the glow of the sunset.

—

The lines to the confessional booths get shorter each year.
Instead, people just wear Pope's costumes.
The lines to the wafer host get shorter each year,
but more people sit down to eat their meals in Pope's costumes.
Fewer people are banned from attending church for a year
for adultery—they just cheat in Pope's costumes
and feel like they've already gone to mass.

Someday the textile companies will realize
that there's nothing they can do about their shortage of fabric
except do away with some popular clothing lines—
and the Pope's costumes' production will stop.

People will continue to be themselves, but in plainclothes.
Even the Pope himself might be reduced to wearing

a rapper's red costume, a prostitute's florid gown
and show up that way on the cable news.
In the windows above, people will turn off their TVs,
turn their cameras on and whisper: "I know this is Paradise!"

On a Red Line Train to Braintree

The first time I saw the Grim Reaper,
he was right next to my foot. I mistook him for an oversize moth.
I was about to squash him but became curious.
He flew up, settled behind the woman
sitting directly in front of me on the train,
and started to inch his scythe toward her neck.
The woman shifted her shoulders.
The Grim Reaper looked quiet and even-keeled.
The passengers next to us saw him too,
but no one did anything and just smiled about it.
There was a poster hanging above the Reaper
with hefty postcards attached, to enroll at a community college.
I considered picking a card and throwing it at him.
That would have caused a disturbance great enough
that the Reaper would have to scram.
But an emotional song was playing in my headphones.
It was too much of a special moment.
Besides, in order to pick up that card
I would have had to lean in too close to the woman,
whose low-cut shirt was not all that well adjusted.
The Reaper never stirred, just inched his scythe closer.
The train came out of the tunnel, and the woman
called her boyfriend to tell him
about the Grim Reaper that hovered behind her.
I was curious whether this would make the boyfriend
break up with her or, on the contrary, offer
new jewelry; but it was too noisy to eavesdrop.
I hoped the woman would exit at the same station as I,
to see if the Reaper would follow her. But she didn't.

I had to go. She remained sitting, blade at her neck.
As I walked out, everyone on the train was commenting on the Grim
      Reaper,
husbands making sophisticated jokes to their wives and children,
translating some of the more difficult stuff for foreigners.
I came home and quickly fell asleep.
I did not dream of anything I had seen.
The next morning, looking through the *Metro* and *Phoenix*,
I looked for news of a subway death—but the papers
must have gone to press too early to run the story.

JOHN J. TRAUSE

Sonnet to the Portuguese

Eu para ti
Tu para mim
Nós para os nossos filhos

Portuguese saying:
inscribed on a platter given
to my father by Jocko

There is a little lower room within
Our house, constructed by the simple art
Of Joaquin DaSilva, from the start
A dear friend of our father, and he's been
A dear friend to us all now and again.
This Jocko, as we call him, does his part
As part of our household at its heart
And adds his punctuations to its din.
Our downstairs house guest need not work too hard:
In minutes by his simple art he's raised
An arbor for the grapevines in the yard,
An elevated porch wholly encased,
Some lofty shelves for books fine to regard,
And then there's so much else for which he's praised.

NOTE: *The epigraph may be translated as "I for you / You for me / We for our children."*

Shakira Shakerata

Ay amor me duele tanto
Me duele tanto
Que te fueras sin decir a donde
Ay amor, fue una tortura perderte

Shakira, "La Tortura" (2005)

chagrin d'amour...

Looking through *tus gafas rosadas*
with the antidote to deadly bigotry being
more, the remedy comes as valeriana trefolia,
a defense against insomnia
on this night of nights, the dual betrayal
of taste and symbol, the red network,
and chance operatives in purple glasses
(Фиоле́товые Очки) at the banquettes.
The chief of operations (*el jefe de operaciones*),
the randy gardener,
sips a shakerato or four, a smoky scotch
on the rocks, as the Nose poses.

Prose flows
like the Danube.

One remembers the amnesia and nostalgia
mingling in the red mist,
the babble and bobbing—so sorry to burst your bubble—
as the plant with the shoulder bag
formed the Baltic Sea out of Балтика beer,
the bottle bursting on the floor in an apartment
in Rutherford, Babel, or Ramsdale, or
at Giverny with the enchanted junta,
nuphar and nymphaea.
You and I are our salt Baltic Sea...

You have the key, the code, the cryptogram and the cipher, coder, don't you?

The wrestler (*luchador*) paws and pauses in between.

As they approached the NKVD and KGB
in 39 steps to success
they were saying goodbye to the Felt Forum
they were saying goodbye to Khmer Rouge
they were saying goodbye to Crimea
they were saying goodbye to Odessa
they were saying goodbye to Valentina Tereshkova
they were saying goodbye to Tai Babilonia
they were saying goodbye to Pina and piña coladas
they were saying goodbye to Campari and Chris Selden
they were saying goodbye to varnishkes and pierogi
they were saying goodbye to small studio space
they were saying goodbye to thespian reverse opportunity,
greeting blackberries and cioppino (or vice versa),
one angel disappeared before the annunciation,
one saint used the bathroom, one danced,
one juggled.

Lighten up. Not me.

Later, in San Francisco.

Meat me.

Pillow Talk

And I   ject of
will be   your pil-
the sub-   low talk

How Beautiful

How beautiful the whip marks on my sex slave's back,
how beautiful the crack of skin, the red, the raw,
so like the red stripes on the U. S. flag,
the contrast of the white and red. How beautiful
the jaw that takes the punch, the maw that takes
me all up to the base in shock and awe.
My bitch, my fag, my leather bag worn raw
with the antidote to deadly bigotry being
more.

How beautifully my sex slave bends down by
the docks, receiving cocks, the payload comes,
set back your clocks as freedom drains into the bay.

How beautiful the day as liberty
is isolate upon the cay. I take
a tortured torch without much of a care
and shove it hard into her derrière,
an accent grave, brave accident à terre.

Prose flows
like the Passaic.

     Blood too…

Fuck you.

Homage to Jasper Johns

Red bar
White bar
Red bar
White bar
Red bar
White bar
Red bar
White bar
Red bar
White bar
Red bar
White bar
Red bar

white star white star white star white star white star white star
white star white star white star white star white star white star
white star white star white star white star white star white star
white star white star white star white star white star white star
white star white star white star white star white star white star
white star white star white star white star white star white star
white star white star white star white star white star white star
white star white star white star white star white star white star

NOTE: *Composed and performed on Tuesday, June 14, 2016, Flag Day.*

ARTHUR RUSSELL

Sharyn

She owned the midday moon above the rock ledge,
steamship smokestack stuck in her lips,
diagonal-zip black leather jacket
open like the chest of a defiant corpse.

She strode
the asphalt path past my window,
long, Colossus-harbor crossers,
owning the sky, the rock ledge, the pale disc moon,
the tough-girl flap of her black leather jacket,

and didn't care—despite the deed to the day
that she carried in her sneer—
for any of it, or the clasp
that held dominion glinting in her hair.

All I ever wanted was to make a breeze
like hers when I walked by.

At the Car Wash

At the car wash, at dawn, the darkness of the plant was almost
suave, a midnight bathroom trip of shadows
along permissive walls.
Sometimes, the dark had a pilot
flickering in the hull of a heater,
exit sign, canvas towel bin glowing in the pallid
grey of skylight. Every morning
for five years. Eighteen hundred mornings,
or we would hear an air leak or water
drip while walking back with our coffee cups

gimbaled between index and thumb—things
we'd need to fix before we opened—and then,
at the electric panel, the knife switch
took a palm to throw, the sequence
of circuit breakers, compressors and fluorescents
satisfied the order etched in our knowing,
and Alan went to hang his army field coat,
and I walked the wash tunnel, collected
license plates and other parts from yesterday,
charmed by rust that bloomed like frost overnight
on the polished steel-plate flooring and washed
away each morning, and Alan came
to grease the bearings, and the white grease pushed
the greasy water out, and, raising garage doors
to put out the signs, I saw the light's progress,
the men arriving, trash cans
empty, money for the register,
hanging card of pine trees in the booth, the tape loop
in the customer walkway selling hot wax to no one.
And then we opened, and the cars came, and the people
nodded to us and stood with crossed arms, watching
steam guns, vacuum wands,
mats flung sideways to the mat rack for a rinse.
And even as we watched, our lives peeled
back one day's layer, shed and
new exposed tomorrow's delicate skin
towards evening.

Flood

This is how the blood swept through the village
of my mother's brain when she woke
at the start of the hemorrhagic stroke
that shoved aside her loves and prejudice
together with her subtle fashion sense

and every index of the orderliness that she professed.

Feeling hot alarm behind her ear,
she pushed the button on the life-alert lanyard,
and the nurse's voice came louder than expected
from the nightstand terminal. I wonder
whether my mother tried to joke with her,
as if to shield the nurse from worry,
as she might have done if my sister had called
on a plain Wednesday;
or whether the flood of blood
had announced its bad intention so doubtlessly
that pleasantries she otherwise insisted on
gave way to frank admission of her fear.

The terminal nurse would have stayed with her
until the ambulance arrived, encouraged her
to drink some water, put her keys in her purse
and unlock the front door now in case,
as it did, it got worse.

And worse, as who she was, and where,
blew black across her mind;
the pantry cans and boxes, row on row
that marked her place, her library of linens,
handbag hooks behind the bedroom door,
perfume bottles bottled up and senseless,
utility bills and annuity statements
in colored files in the lower, left-hand drawer
of the desk that faced the Intercoastal Waterway,
blew black across her mind;

the boy with the cleft palate who called her Tulip,
the cigarette ashes they tipped in her girlfriend's shoes,
the green and black tiles in Sylvia's bathroom;
laughing at a comic in the Catskills with her sister,

the fake fox fur that her husband banished from his car,
and the bitter refrain of marriage blew black across her mind;
the part that liked butter cookies and hot, black coffee
and crossword puzzles blew black across her mind.

When we arrived that afternoon
like three un-Magi,
children, grown, with failures of our own to tend,
to find her washed up on that hospital bed,
with breathing tubes and a wedding ring,
and monitors creating the illusion of the life
that had already tumbled from her body,

my sister at the bedside held her hand,
IV and all. I took pictures of the names
of drugs written in marker on the velvety drips;
and my little brother, in a folded-forward slump,
sat in a chair, further from the curtain, and cried.

And so we attended till the hospice lady came,
and then, we were ourselves again.

Andrea from Burlington

That more than heart, that hearth,
her ribs and breast which,
powder-warm, one summer night,
she lay in breathing love beside my own,

        became my home.

That pillow-hogging, thuggish hair
in ginger skeins
that tangled, long, and lazy framed her
fair and forest-thick-with-freckles face,

and promised grace.

The long, untangled length
of arms with narrow wrists
as pale as fresh-barked branches,
crossed on knees as fingers droop

on my front stoop.

Her quarter-sawn and copper-flecked,
cambium-quick and morning-fresh,
ocean, olive, autumn, yielding,
furious, green as mossy fieldstone eyes:

my enterprisc.

Her dimpled chin, peninsular
like Florida from soft, pink lips
descending to Caribbean conflicts
she would meddle,
even fight a naval war to win. That point:

her queenest joint.

If not that we had battled
black as rifle butts for love,
seething, head on, harsh as frozen needle spray
thrown back in winter cheeks
from river-crashing cannonballs,

and damned it all;

that hair, those eyes, those arms, that chin,
that heart, that hearth, that battle black,
that leaving lost, I would again,

I would again the autumn
of her red hair enter,
wet with rain, and yet still burning:

one more turning.

Excursion

Until you,
my hours stayed on the clock face,
and my loyalties under the hand
over my heart.

There were no spring snakes in a can.
My skin was just a thing
to keep my heart dry.

While we watched
a gull
pull apart
a Big Mac box
in an Indiana parking lot,
you became my cheeks,
and I, the vaulting boy;

and I was the rock
to tell the crumpled sheet
that scissors broke, and we were free to love.

But who will dog me home
from this excursion?

The moon, for all the tides might pull,
yet in tethers, heeds the Earth.

MELANIE KLEIN

Untraversable

In the elevator, no one looks, or every
one looks covertly, peripherally,
observing unwritten protocol.

Different when a train pulls up:
glazed-eyed riders stare openly
at those waiting on the platform,
at the ones not boarding this train,
who stare unflinchingly back
across the chasm. We and they
inhabit different dimensions,
ride different vectors; we are
of different species, even phyla,
one terrestrial and one aquatic,

and neither the fact that
recently they were us, nor
that soon we will be them,
makes the slightest difference.

The Ramp

New angle, chair by porch door,
reveals at last how the bluebird,
each flight from apple tree outpost
to her house, does it: how each
winged *thwump* presses down hard
a great wedge of air against the earth,

thwump,

        grounds her, bucks her up and forward,
pulsing, propulsing,
                    thwump,

lifting her, building beneath her
each time, every,
          all that way   to the chittering

babes (*thwump*)

this invisible ramp
of solid   air,
solid   love.

The Cafeteria Lady

The cafeteria lady sings something inhuman,
radical evolution of some Gospel tune,
and tends to the ketchup and mustard
while the first customers stumble in
and sit among the herded tables.

The crumbs stand high and stark
in the low-angled sun, casting shadows
that stretch along the formica
toward her high and warbly tone,
her cryptic arrhythmia.

Most of the people have earbuds in
or talk, loudly, to flush out the last
of night's darkness, but when some
depart and leave one alone, or in that
space between their funneled tunes,

her song pierces an awareness
who turns, then, to look around
for the source of her unearthly sound.

In the New Darkness

Since the blindness had begun,
the old idea had breached,
had embarked on a zigzagging path
through his consciousness, stopping only
to put on different clothes, as if for sleep,
and kill time with a slow, wan dance
until he woke again.

Now undistracted by his surroundings,
he found he could catch glimpses,
from different angles: the idea
lumbering through his awareness.
It was crudely shaped, he saw,
and savage in manner, its dark lobes
dragging heavily against his thoughts.

Not wanting to disturb or frighten it,
he worked to manifest as absence,
hanging back in the shadowed corners
of himself, until he sensed that the scans
of its filmy eye had passed over him.

He wondered about the reality of this,
of hiding within his mind from
something of its own substance, but
in the new darkness it felt real enough,
and, in these forgotten corners,
other images stirred, rose up,
brushed against him as they passed.

STUART LEONARD

Iron Will

She had an iron will,
a black bar
wrought with stubborn,
cold to the touch,
but you could see
the molten core
in her eyes,
ready to spit.

Sometimes the black bar
would cage you,
because it was iron,
because it could.

You shrank in there
until you were small enough
to crawl out,

only to find her
caged in that iron,

and being caged out
was as bad as being caged.

She could beat you with that bar
until the pain didn't matter,
until you didn't care,
could grab the coming blow
and laugh at those smoldering eyes.

There was no bend in it,
only break you

or break itself.

Rust won,
ate away the iron,
left a pile of anemic dust,

her molten eyes gone dim,
the black bar
a shadow she waves

Tooth

Betrayed by his daughters, my grandfather railed.
His wrists and ankles strapped to the bed
by thick padded belts. He pulled in vain
at the restraints, spit obscenities at his captors.

His eyes bulged from a frail head
that lolled on a skeleton draped with pale flesh.
I couldn't believe this feeble man wrestled a needle
from the brawny nurse and tossed it across the room.

He rejected the treatments, refused to eat,
willed this in one last great stubborn act.
Though the prognosis was optimistic,
he had no interest in the cure.

The sisters whispered at the foot of the bed
as the patriarch settled, mumbling softly.
I heard them speak of Goldie, his wife of sixty years,
how he would be with her soon.

My mom and I just cleaned out the apartment
we moved him into two years before.
The same food we moved sat in the cabinets.
He never opened the toaster my aunt bought him.

His arm strained at the belt, his withered hand
reached out, fingers pinched, face calmer.
Take it—he gasped—Take it, it's yours.
I looked at the empty fingers waving in the air.

Fingers waving in the air, pinching a lost tooth, my first.
A taste of blood where a moment before
the stubborn tooth dangled. Grandpa looking down,
with brown, wavy hair, a knowing smile.

Just before dinner, he asked to see the loose incisor,
brought me downstairs to his dentist office
and made to examine the tooth. He snatched it out,
quick as a thief, then offered it back to me.

I worried that my grandfather had cheated,
that my tooth had not legitimately fallen out,
so the tooth fairy would punish this transgression
and withhold her nocturnal gift.

The tooth between us, I smell dinner,
the exam room, the musk of sleeping pipes
in a rack on his desk. I reach for the lost tooth.
My grandmother calls from upstairs.

How to Make an American Name

Take an ancient Hebrew name.
Settle in promised land.
Exile and return. Repeat.
Then exile.
Let it linger in a foreign city.
Babylon, Alexandria, Antioch, as needed.
Allow a fallen empire or two,
a jihad, a crusade.

Migrate north.
Pick up some Greek.
Convert the Khazars.
Watch them fall.
Make the appropriate adjustments.
Add Cyrillic and Slav.
Move a little north, a little east.
Farm in land of Russ.
Let sit a few centuries in Russian brine.
Should have at least twelve consonants,
no more than three vowels.
A pogram or two or three is normal.
Escape west.
Disembark at Ellis Island.
Irish immigration officer
should gag on twelve consonants, three vowels.
Allow officer to revise into his name,
as revised by the English.
Starts with an *L*, there's an *e* and *n*,
so, similar.
Take to lower east side.
Work in sweat shop.
Make it to suburbs.
Blend.

1974

The new drug awareness lectures worked.
Thanks to the pictures they showed us,
we were well-aware of what drugs
to pilfer from our parents.
Bennies or barbs,
we could make an informed choice.

Nobody was dead yet, or even in jail.

If the cops caught you with weed,
you could watch them smoke it,
later, behind the bowling alley.

When Sachs was back in town,
we could cop some real acid
on little paper squares
embossed with a caricature of Tricky Dick.

Even our block-busted town,
our shut down, their side, our side town,
was transformed by the blotter on your tongue.
Ernie and me sat on the curb for three hours
while the neon sign of the Blue Ribbon Inn
desperately tried to tell us something.

We just found ourselves
wandering down the overgrown side rail
to the abandoned Frisbee factory,
toward the sound of Zeppelin
blasting from the cassette player
that never left home without Roger.

Most of our fathers
were shit-faced in the Lyon's Den.
Our mothers were at home with Valium
and Mary Tyler Moore.

The tape rolled from one wheel to another.
Roger turned it over and hit play.

In that hall of broken windows
where the outlines from scrapped machines
scarred the floor like the chalk marks
of a crime scene, we drank and danced
and smoked and sang.

MICHAEL O'BRIEN

Back Story

I am not trying to tell it straight
because, like life, the story does not
go straight; it sleeps and seeps
with the real and the imagined.

Sometimes a light touch can lift
a heavy subject. We need to care less,
sleep more, and laugh often.

The rocks holding the hill against
itself will always tumble down,
but there is no rush to push them back
into position.

The rain will always wash debris
onto the lawn's edge; the deck will
always need a power wash and new stain.

As it must, fixing a backed-up toilet
is intensely necessary and immediate.
Eventually, everything works itself out.

I am not a constant gardener, but
I do like volunteer flowers and birds
who do their own thing without
taunting me too much.

Double Helix

I once mocked a student
who wrote the line, "Rabbits eat
upon the lawn." I said,
"Where the hell else are they
going to eat, the Waldorf Astoria?"

She went on to become a fine poet
and a life-long friend.
But now, I have rodents
eating upon my deck.

The squirrels dig up almost
forgotten nuts from
our backyard hill,
bring them to the top step
of the deck and leave shell
fragments everywhere.

Now that spring is here,
I sweep off this residue daily.

I don't understand rodent behavior,
but it echoes mouse DNA,
of which humans share 90%,
but we don't shit where we eat;
at least I try not to.

Forgotten Things

I lost the name of the actress
in that commercial; she was once
the girlfriend of Tony Romo.

I once stashed the mallard decoy
my father made inside the cat's
playhouse, which he never used.
We lost him to old age and degenerative
nerve disease. Three years later,
I looked for the decoy to put atop
a new bookcase but couldn't find it.

I reviewed culprits who might have
taken the duck, workers, visitors, friends.
I found the decoy inside the cat house
when I went to move it to make room
for my wife's upstairs office.

Things float into and out of mind
with a rhythm that is beyond my control.
My mother lost her mind, and later life,
to Alzheimer's, the ultimate forfeit.

The things that go missing in the wormhole
of gravity waves make me both villain and victim.
I have been to four funerals this summer,
so the losses have been mounting up.

On Stage

The franchise of my life
has been a saga, a series
of escapades that perpetuated
bad behavior and weak punchlines
but delivered by amusing hints
of action to come.

Looking back brings, of course,
a nostalgia which plays memory
of sour acceptances and refuge
in an imagined magical doom.

The allegory swings from
slapstick to bloodshed and beyond
directed by a perverse sense of
cruel tribute to prosthetic smiles.

One Trip at a Time

My story must sustain itself
all the way to a twisty finish.

This stamina may not make much sense,
but an unreliable narrator doesn't falter
in his commitment to absurdity.

What is handy for expression comes
to remarkable intrigue or action,
a depiction of the creative process.

It ends tense with hostility, suspicion
and a hidden agenda.

I asked her what she wanted
to do, wash my feet or type,
as I can no longer do either.

DON ZIRILLI

Red

You eat the chocolate
before the wine.
You want no color
on that deep delight,
no blood in the shadows.

Or is it the wine first,
to heed every accent,
the onset of the aftertaste,
curve of glass
caressing curve of mouth,
while chocolate waits
to ease you with
its imitation of night
from the pinch
of this waking world?

I'm not sure
because I alternate,
a bite of one,
a sip of the other,
a winking communion,
a dance from floor to wall
and back again,
as Donald O'Connor would do,
the virtuoso
of not quite falling
and not quite getting up.

Ghost

Something moves the reeds,
nudges your shirt off the porch rail.

A black bird on the pier.
I think of telling you.
It's gone.

I feel your hand on my back
and, expecting your face at my shoulder,
I turn my head.

I have never been to this inlet before,
but I have seen this water.

Mosquito

Your wizened cry, your many pleas,
summon me to anguished wariness,
to know your wish to kiss, lips unnoticed,
your moans for wine, your briny teeth sunk deep
to the brink of an itch, a chaste sixteenth of an inch
now violated, your roses raking my skin.

Why do you want me? Why? You hover,
drop to pierce me, rise, ignite the stitch
of greased affliction with your spit. You sing
almost notes, like she struck, silencing.

Fugue

You told me once how you'd get stuck in patterns
like passing trees in car windows, or linoleum tiles.

You tried to turn away your eyes, but you were
frozen and helpless, like a yearbook smile.

Last night, someone kissed my eyes three times,
and, on my back, she scratched a broken cross.

Now I'm looking drowsily at a bathroom floor
I've never seen before, descending to its rhythm, lost.

Made of Gauze

My mother, made of gauze, could never be
unveiled, for veils she was, and to be viewed
she must be worn, as oysters wear the sea
around their pearly necks, though born as nude
as teardrops on a cheeky smile, in wrecks
of bone and coral, over collars getting
wet. My mother, softly woven hex
upon a silent story, not regretting,
never passing, only waving, blanket
blanking lovers, love absorbing, warmly
nothing, beautiful as wind, so plank it,
stand in salty air, the plankton forming
dusty pillows, as their cases trail
behind. *I'm empty. Let me be your sail.*

FRANCES LOMBARDI-GRAHL

I'm Not Afraid of Paterson

I was mugged here twice
but never slain.
Once I even got my wallet back.

My uncle was mugged here too
in front of his insurance office on 10th Avenue
but never moved to East Paterson
despite my mother's warnings
that he'd lose his life if he didn't.

It was here I had my first kiss
behind a stack of reference books
at the main library

and here where I wrote my first poem
though it had nothing to do with Ginsberg or the Great Falls.

I'm not afraid of Paterson,
unlike my husband from the Bronx,
or my cousins from Hillside
who compared her to Newark
one spring afternoon when we walked past the lovely St. John's
        Cathedral.

Many have warned me not to come here at night,
or to carry pepper spray if I absolutely had to come,
but I'm not afraid of Paterson,
city of my parents and grandparents,
city that has kept my dreams flourishing
like wildflowers rising from the cracks of her mean streets.

My Mother's Hands

My mother's hands were rarely idle.
They used to make things like comforters and bundt cakes.
Sometimes her hands reminded me of birds,
their wings fluttering above her crochet needles,
bright yarn encircling her fingers.

In a black and white photo,
my mother's hands are holding my infant body
half hidden under a plaid blanket.
In another, they're encircling my father's neck
as she kisses him on the cheek and smiles into the camera's eye.

I've seen my mother's hands
buried in bread dough and soapsuds,
covered in flour white as a magician's hands.

She wore only one ring,
but most of the time her fingers were bare
because they were always moving,
beginning as a child when she packed crayons
into Crayola boxes that slid along conveyor belts.

Those hands sewed buttons on women's winter coats,
and carried trays to hospital rooms
where they opened milk cartons and packets of salt.

Those hands were rarely folded.
They stitched, scrubbed, chopped, and kneaded,
then moved to the rhythm of her crochet needles.

My mother always hated idle hands.
She used to tell me they were the devil's best friends.

Beginning

On the fourth day of the new year,
I return to the beginning:
the alphabet, numbers,
the calendar, the clock.

My tongue stumbles through a list of foreign names
they've already begun to change.

I ask about their countries,
and they show me panoramas of cities and towns
on their cell phones,
showing off their mountains and deserts,
even their towers, steeples and domes

Next, they step in front of the class
and find their countries on the map,
then write their names on post-its
which they place inside their countries,

and the world that had seemed so distant and huge
fits into our room
like the flag in the corner
with its stripes and stars.

MICHAEL MANDZIK

To MARION of LION'S TEETH

1.

The Muse, um, lives where she breathes,
where she folds and kneads her forms
drawn in spirit, sown and shorn
of naught but best intentions.
She does not fill vine
with grape so that wine
might mull or craft purpose
solely from need.
Her wanton mysteries daze,
from deeper in her lair,
out from *unter den Linden*.
She sparks, he thinks:
what would come if I cut this branch
and graft it thus, to the trunk? If I poked
this seed up in her womb,
what would come? Might it bloom?

2.   <u>Moving On</u>
Our first direction that morning
was into Reverse.
Slowly,
chopped livers shivered,
iced into buckets by frozen shovels.
Missed you barely through
the bottom holes.
You kicksparked the clock
forward into warmer time zones
with cooler latitudes.
Wow that's great, you said,
now shift into Drive
and step on the gas.

3.

Every day is Mother's Day
but especially in late Spring,
the month after forsythias
scream at me to clean up my room,
the month after my Mom's birthday,
when azaleas have popped out of buds,
when dogwoods' white veils wed young green trees,
when brilliant maroon Japanese maples
leave us warm in nurturing photons.

4.

One long task remains before me.
My clever heart is cluttered,
cleaving to all I would
clean from my veins.
My roots drill blind
in the cavity of the past.

Thirty-one years have gone,
pewtered frames of windows, passed.
Burdens buried with hopes of heaven
and you, my dearest mother still,
I could not hold you here.

Your happy laughter,
your screeched delight when
fits of sneezing caught you
breathless, left you gasping,
just about cackling, smiling.

You'd say, "It's the histamines!"
as you giggled into your napkin.
"Red wine has histamines,

---

and it's histamines make me sneeze!"

Your breathless smile, always wide
and open, like your arms akimbo,
welcoming any and everyone to your table,
your giving of thanks, for life,
for joy, for all to share.
Your smile left, you, breathless.

5.

Some days I fear that there are
more dandelions than Mandziks.
Wadded spores age all too well.
Draggly thickneck rootage drills
unfoiled until feastwaters feed
capillarily forky green leaves,
wider than their longest sides, resting
soaked in wattage purely spread,
direct, or ambient, shaded, or
even all fogged up. Tragically,
there are in the world, some days,
more dandelions than Mandziks.

Suit Department Karma

1.
As far back as I can remember, nothing ever fit me right.
My pant cuffs were rolled up inside
like the too-big waist band,
tacked to my size with a few stitches.
My shirt sleeves got tucked up,
sewed so the cuffs just covered my wrists.
It looked like I had stripes between the elbows
and cuffs. And of course, the cuffs were folded back
and buttoned. One of my aunts puffed me up when she told me,

"When well-to-do men wore their shirts like this, they were called
     French cuffs."
Then one day, I learned this wasn't so. It can still take a while for
     truth to find me.
Moving along slow and steady, this is how it usually gets to me.
After which, it drops on me like a bushmaster from a tree.

2.
We all wear the scarf of regret.
Ants flattened underfoot while bringing food to the colony.
The last cigarette crushed in a tray. Lives, stubbed out of place,
yet not out of mind. Ashy residue floats from a smoking barrel.
Hand-made muffler collars chilled remembrance.
This silent wrap may not be entirely appropriate for swimwear.
Even more unthinkable is to be caught without it,
an unmentionable accessory to naked truth.

3.
for Ronald Eric Schreiber

The Milky Way
is permanent press,
meant to be lived in.
So how's the fit?
It's all in the way
that you treat people.
If done wrong,
the look is crumpled.
When it's done right,
you look like you belong.
Of course, some wrinkles are free,
comfortably on purpose.

Backspace

I need a day, at least
one day per week to sort
my bags of mental change
from fields of crumpled bills,

But that day must fall
before the wrens of Saturn
wring blood from stones
or heave the wrongs of Spring
and all is lost in a stack of needles.

The pitchfork with its twisted tine
holds the sea infrequent,
tunes a sextant,
flattens atonality.

Start on the last page.
Read from now to then.
Interject the leavened pages,
risen, folded, knead connection.

If A, then B,
no truer thought be told.

Logos cubes our final view,
streams Creation under dome
until Whispers crack agenda,
and Fictation roots our soul.

That dimension is no longer,
did not linger for a second.
The allied past is passed; has left us.
We are stuck here, future-struck.

DELLA ROWLAND

Poem of No Return

She sat down to write the poem of no return
in front of the window that
squared off a piece of greenish night.

Rain sheeted the pane,
and from one lightning stroke to the next,
the night dissolved,
except for the reflected room,
the first few outside steps,
and the glaring white gravel driveway.

She began to solidify on the window screen
like the huge tan moth battering to reach the light.

As the poem began to come, a car came also.

Up the white driveway,
bracing the rain and lightning increasing,
it came straight and silent on the silver gravel,
through the window and over the watery desk.

Her dead lovers climbed out of the car.
Her live ones lined up alongside.
As they looked at her from the living room,
for the life of her she could not tell
which were live or dead,
or which she had loved more,
or not at all.

So she gathered them all to her poem of no return,
laying them end to end on the silver sliver of road
that stretched and shrank

beyond the window's boundary.

Then she sighed, and,
like the huge tan moth,
sank down beside the light.

Don McNary's Office

I know you are approaching down the hall
by keys and coins jingling, crisp footsteps,
the decisive swishes of jacket lining.

Sitting next to you in the small office,
the smell of soap seeps through even your wool suit,
the same smell of some summer nights
lying in the big bed at your mama's house
under open windows.

Don McNary describes how changing
some procedures slightly
will lighten our case loads and move
clients quicker through the system.

I could describe how your brown skin
lightens slightly from face to shoulder
beneath collar and shirt buttons,
and how long, long muscles
quicken beneath skin
like current lies beneath water.

Gene Pool

A sad ruined river runs
through my father's side.

I walked fast on thin ice
my whole life
to not fall through.

The river's source
—a spring—seemed
not enough to drown in,

but a falls fell steep,
and the mouth emptied
into vast waters deep.

Now I swim fast every day,
muddy laps toward the rim
of the earth, Diana Nyad
stroking through the sharks
and cold waves,
going for the other side.

ADDIE MAHMASSANI

Fingerprints of Fools

The boy at the bar
buys us shots of tequila.
Before I even swallow mine,
I'm gonna throw up.

These are the highest heels
in Midtown,
but you bet I can still run.

Cheap sports bar glass door with no character,
sweet summer city air,
fingerprints of fools
who've entered or left this place.

Inside, they're flashing rings.
Engaged girls are diamond peacocks
whose plumes have closed in
around one man.
We're taken, they say,
fluttering and fanning their fingers.

She, in her fake tiara and veil,
pokes her head out the door.
Wearing white,
she's glowing!
She's glowing in the light
of the TVs!

Can you come kiss this guy?
He wants a kiss
for the tequila!

Why? I groan,
hunched over myself.

For the tequila!
He's Mexican!
He wants to kiss an American!

Why not? I groan.

Sober up, lady.
This
is your moment.

Cheap Midtown sports bar glass door with no character,
sweet summer city air,
fingerprints of fools
who've entered or left this place.

I swing it open,
and the crowd parts,
and the boy who bought us the tequila
is there, waiting,
waiting for me
in my slutty black dress,
and my highest high heels.

I hear you wanna kiss an American?

He has no time to answer
because I have walked the aisle
and grabbed him,
and I am giving him
exactly what he wanted.

He dips me way back

and raises a hand,
the way grooms sometimes do,
and we, in the war dance
of the truly lonely,
the truly free,
make
this
stupid bar
amazing.

Woodstock

It was a perfect half moon,
and you were a perfect
half love.

It was your kind of night,
mossy spring drizzle,
a man in a window,
playing flamenco guitar.

The soft slate roof
of the pale blue carriage house
was curving in.

You said
they should fix it.
I said I liked it that way.

Little beads of water
lined the branchy maze above us
crisscrossing the moon,
quiet and still,
the way you like it.

The ground felt
so flat.

I wanted
to have sex.
You wanted
to have a cigarette.

We settled for sleeping
in each other's arms.

Just tonight.
Please,
just tonight.

ELINOR MATTERN

Thank You for Your Condolences. But...

If you know what it's like to lose
your father, and it was terrible,
or you imagine that it would be,

and will be terrible when you do,
because you love him so much,
he is your sheltering tree,

you are not operating in the same
emotional matrix as someone like me,
who lost my father when I was two,

and five, and seven and twelve,
and fifteen and twenty-two,
and a hundred times in each of those years,

and all the ones in between.
I lost the word "father" when he crushed
the little crescent that was me

in his hands. Again. And again.
And then got on a plane at Idlewild
bound for Rio and Quito and Fes.

Sent postcards from Marrakesh and Maricá
with no return address.

Love Song

The dead know what time it is
all the time. The dead know snow

from the inside out. The dead know
the taste of the clouds and that

breathing isn't enough. But the dead
have forgotten how a word is a sound

and now they have only the language
of sky. They know the temperature

of midnight, and that rain can't live
without trees. The dead know cold

is not the opposite of hot. The dead
know that tears aren't salt by accident.

We can't live without knowing, and
the dead know that knowing

doesn't fix it all. And the dead know
that the risk of drowning is the price

of crawling from the sea.

Across the Sea, Water and Glass

I am holding a blue bottle in my hands
in the Rosetta Café in Rome.

Always the bottle is blue. Aquamarine days.
Looking at the world through blue eyes.

Navy blue nights, the glass cobalt, clear,
water-colored. But water has no color,

reflects what holds it, contains it, opposes it.
A bottle the color of the late day sky, cool,

smooth in the hand, air bubbles, tiny bumps,
the pontle mark, the scar where the glassblower's rod

was torn away. How does the total opacity of sand
melt like this, transmute into translucence?

In the Restaurant Rainer Maria Rilke in Prague,
sunlight glinting off glass, the carafe, blue,

heavy in my hand, curved, solid. Water outside
the window. Vlatava River. The Charles Bridge.

GIL FAGIANI

Waterfall

Marine recruiters
in mud-brown blouses
wait at the bottom of the stairs
of the Atlantic Avenue subway station
for young men to tumble down like salmon from a waterfall.

The Marines
cast their nets:
"Yo, stud . . . college degree,
cash advance, your own home, exotic pussy."

Leaving out:
lopped-off limbs,
sand storm psychosis,
barbecued kids, booby-trapped corpses.

Seeds

Pennsylvania Military College

I find a recipe in an anarchist magazine
on how to hallucinate using household products,
buy twelve packets of morning glory seeds:
six of Heavenly Blues, and six of Pearly Gates.
The salesman asks what a cadet wants with flower seeds.
I tell him I'm the Commandant's aide-de-camp,
and it's for his garden.

A chemistry major grinds the seeds,

and I pack the powder into triple X gelatin capsules.
My buddies laugh at me at the Sun City Bar
when I flash my stash of hallucinogens,
but join me in washing the caps down
with 15-cent drafts of Pabst Blue Ribbon.

An hour later, at the Friday frat mixer,
I see a cadet walking across a row of chairs,
arms out, another stumbling into the band
as the drummer solos on "Wipe Out,"
and a third on his knees, clinging
to the legs of a Haverford sorority sister.

Fonzi

An anonymous call directs the police to a white Cadillac Coupe de Ville burning near the abandoned Washburn Wire Factory, by East 115th Street and the East River. Inside the trunk, they find a human torso, with its asshole blown out by a cherry bomb. After a search of the car and the surrounding area, the cops can't locate the head or limbs but inside the stomach, the Medical Examiner discovers teeth and IDs Alfonso "Fonzi" Dini. He's rumored to be the main man, cutting pure heroin with lactose—milk sugar—for the Italian wholesalers who operate out of social clubs and apartments along Pleasant Avenue. He's known to be meticulous, blending quarter-kilo and half-kilo packages without a trace of powder on the floor or sink drain. Two greedy narcos begin to tail Fonzi, demanding an increase in their payoffs. Fonzi is a tough old bird who boasts of many "dead bodies" in his past. When he refuses, they plant two ounces in the trunk of his de Ville and arrest him. Before he puts up money for Fonzi's bail, Don "One Ball" Sebastiano rushes to Fonzi's motel lab to check for loose packages, and realizes his master mix-man has been skimming a quarter kilo off every kilo he cut.

WAYNE L. MILLER

Until Then

Standing on this river bank in the morning fog, I can see nearby
waves, but only larger waves rise in the distance. Sunlight burns
through—rapid glint scatters the surface. The revealed far shore seems
like here—trees, boulders, gravel, but not being there, I do not know
for sure. I can walk the bridge across, but its span is five miles North,
and then I must walk five miles South, arriving hours older, in
different light, perhaps covered in fog or freezing rain. I could swim,
but then I would be otherwise changed—wet, tired, looking at a
distance which is now near, using memory to compare. She is neither
here nor there, but somewhere else, and I must wait until we can hold
each other again. She told me, *until then*, and walked away. I can look
for her in the distant weeks, and from there, I can reflect back to this
lonely day, but unlike mere water, I cannot cross time.

Stationery Store

Red Bull in the cooler, five-hour drinks on the counter, lottery tickets
and cigarettes behind me, Penthouse on the top rack, herbal tea on the
corner shelf, ATM near the door, coffee canisters by the pastry bins.

When I was a kid, we called this place Pop's Candy Store. Pops sold it
to me twenty years ago, and I changed the name to Park Street
Stationery. I sold Mars bars, baseball cards, Twinkies, Pez dispensers,
even pens and paper. I ask myself—when did I become a drug and
porn dealer? When did I start running a numbers racket?

I never changed the sign. It still says stationery, candy, cigars. I
haven't sold cigars in fifteen years. No one buys them anymore.

People come in for their fix—coffee to wake up, Red Bull to stay up,
lottery tickets to feel hopeful, cigarettes to feel calm, sugar to fill a
craving, herbal tea to sleep, porn for immediate use. I know what my

regular customers need by looking at their eyes when they're in the line. That saves me some time.

Last week, I signed with a delivery service. They text me orders and send a guy with a van. Next month, I'll hire some kid after school to pack boxes. I'll tell him, keep away from the drugs, the gambling, the porn, don't feel dirty about the product, don't think about the customers or their families. Just put the blue gloves on, pack the damn boxes, cash your paycheck, and wash your hands before you go home. There isn't much room for sympathy in this business.

DAVIDSON GARRETT

The Night Before Christmas Eve: Germany, 1970

For Leslie

Advent darkness. Determined stars sneak through
tiny breaks of swirling cloud cover, hovering over
West Berlin. A walled city, decorated with simple
holly & greens, unwilling to sanction holiday

overkill during chilled rhetoric of Cold War.
Two eighteen-year-olds from Louisiana,
a closeted homosexual & a Carol Burnett *wannabe*—
thespians on a college-sponsored USO tour,

rejoice in their new-found freedom; adolescent troubles
frozen till January's return. Chance or misfortune
conducts this performance of youth's final cabaletta.
Burning the pocket of the young male, tickets for

the Deutsche Opera's traditionally-staged *Tosca*,
we navigated through mink coats & men in leather,
the bug-eyed hicks climbing to the nosebleed section
of a surprisingly modern theater. As the soprano

finishes her aria, *Vissi d'arte*, the enthusiastic
Americans scream, "Brava Diva!" Foreign commentary
scorned by German etiquette—as gruff voices declare:
"heathens im haus"—erupting belly laughter heard

far beyond barbed wire. A swift curtain call escape!
Puccini's lyrical drama—fueled ravenous appetites,
strolling along the Kurfürstendamm, past the historic
Kaiser-Wilhel Gedächtniskirche, its bombed steeple

a reminder of the horrors of World War Two
nestled in the sliced-heart of an occupied metropolis.
Signs on café after café read: *Geschlossen*. Weary limbs,
growling stomachs—until a neon Kriss Kringle glows

above an open beer garden. Steak, sausage,
schnitzel, sauerbraten, potatoes & ice cream:
the first course gobbled near the stroke of 2 a.m.
Afterward, a Mercedes taxi driven by a native

with a broken compass—delivers Hansel & Gretel
to an aluminum dormitory, courtesy of the U.S. Army.
On this stark night, friendship's fleeting light
will be transformed into a sweet operatic memory.

A Yuletide gift for the songless years to come.

The Mock Turtle & Me

Beautiful Soup, so rich and green
Waiting in a hot tureen!
Who for such dainties would not stoop?
Soup of the evening, beautiful Soup!
         —Lewis Carroll

At eight years old, after surviving
the prim & proper Eisenhower fifties,
I found myself elated, joyous—
acting in a children's theater troupe,
an ambitious, pint-sized thespian
born with drive & determination.
I became the Mock Turtle
for this amateur production
of the fantastical *Alice In Wonderland*,
a theatrical diversion
to enhance mundane days

---

living in an oppressive segregated city
nestled in the northwest corner
of Bible-thumping Louisiana.
My co-actors, southern-accented
boys & girls, created timeless characters
Charles Dodgson's imagination invented,
decked-out in bright dancing tights
fitted snugly under cartoon-like apparel,
a visual kaleidoscope of make-believe—
our escape from the blue-collar world
we were unfortunately destined to inhabit.
Weeks before, my devoted mother
constructed an elaborate tortoise costume
designed from her rhapsodic mind.
Nimble fingers lovingly sculpted
the hard chelonian shell
using two yards of chicken wire
covered by canvas potato sacks
dyed chocolate-brown. This concoction
attached to a cinnamon-colored
female bathing suit
fronted by stitched-squares
stuffed with fistfuls of foam rubber
to represent the turtle's belly—
giving it a padded reptilian look.
To complete my creature attire,
my legs stretched into gray leotards
embellishing tubby thighs
as my freckled face absorbed
gobs of green greasepaint
with thick mascara
highlighting innocent eyes—
evoking a portrait of melancholy.
In my entrance scene, with scuba diving
flippers cushioning flabby feet, I waddled
onto the stage to greet curious Alice

standing beside the winged Gryphon.
I planted myself firmly, dead center under
the spotlighted proscenium arch.
With practiced falsetto, I began my lament
in a dirge-like tempo mingled with sobs:
Soup Soup, Beautiful Soup. Beautiful Beautiful Soup.
And from that moment on, I've never returned to reality.

Not So Clear-Eyed

"I think I'm in the early stages
of Fuchs dystrophy," my sister whines
over long distance. "It's a degenerative

eye disease, affecting the endothelium
which maintains proper
fluid in the cornea." A mouthful

for my brain to absorb
through cell phone static.
"And by the way,"

my ophthalmologist
tells me—"you'll probably
develop this condition too—

it's highly genetic."
Perhaps that explains
the blinding glare

magnifying morning light
as I walk to buy the newspaper
at the newsstand. Or the rainbows

around red lights & streetlights

---

glimmering after dark. Or the
squinty impressionistic vision

I experience on awakening
most days, until the ashen
cloudiness dissipates.

Just one more misery
to list on my long list
of aging issues.

At the Frick Museum, I ponder
J. M. W. Turner's watercolor,
Chateau de Dieppe.

A fusion of delicate pink,
yellow & blue pastels
dominated by radiant sunglow

as if this French port city
is being cleansed & redeemed
by hallowed beams from heaven.

Brown etchings of structures
faintly emerge through splashed
white brush strokes—

a lone castle on a hill
looms vaguely, almost formless
through the abstract atmosphere

painted on paper. I wonder
if this British artist suffered
from Fuchs dystrophy too?

KEN VENNETTE

Dead Leon

Leon wasn't always dead.
He was very much alive when he decided
he was the leader of our pack:
troublemakers, 13 or 14 years old, who hung out
on the corner of Church and Main.
Not necessarily looking for guidance.

Leon, at thirty or more, wore
greased-back hair and cowboy boots—
a cross between Elvis and The Man in Black.
Tarnished false teeth highlighted
his imbecilic gaze.

He led us down the paths of childish tomfoolery.
We followed like sheep behind the shepherd,
frozen by fear to his wishes and dictates.

On a hot night in August, he led the way
as we walked the two miles to the drive-in.
He had us knock on random doors,
then run like the dickens
before the people answered,
or scream obscenities at passing cars.

In the ultimate show of superiority,
he pointed toward the fanciest house in town,
at the shiny glass globe on its pedestal
centered on the lawn: "Double dare me!
I'll kick that fuckin' ball in a million pieces."

We dared.
He kicked.

It exploded.

We ran so hard we could hardly breathe
when we met up in the brush lot east
of the drive-in. We showered him
with obligatory adoration,
at the same time fearing to be found out.
We moved on toward the movies
as long shadows grew into darkness.

"You little fuckers follow me.
I know the best way," he said.
We followed.

We were almost there, then
the snapping, crunching noise
as the bear trap grabbed his leg,
snapped it like a twig.

We all ran, left him there
wailing in the night.
We crashed through the brush in the dark,
distanced ourselves from the sirens
and flashing lights,
wondering how to sneak home—
undetected.

We avoided him in the weeks that followed,
free of his cruel dominance.
He was effectively dethroned.

The following winter,
Leon backed into a snow bank,
unknowingly plugged the tailpipe.
He left the car running for warmth.
I don't recall the woman's name,

but she was said to be a whore.
Both were asphyxiated
in the middle of a blow job.
They died
with it still in her mouth.

The prevailing conclusion,
at least among the boys in town:
"What a way to go."

Currant Berry Jam

Visitors saw the currant berries
by the old barn down the road.
They offered brother Mike and me
a dollar each to go pick a bunch
so they could make currant berry jam.

We walked the half mile and went into
the cow barn to ask the old farmer.
There was Annie, the forty-something
retarded daughter, nonchalantly
drowning kittens in a stainless steel milk pail.
Mike and I stopped and watched.

She kept shooing the meowing mother cat away.
There were ten or twelve kittens in a cardboard box
with their eyes barely open. She looked up at us
with her crossed eyes and rotten-tooth smile.
"Doin' chores," she said.

She was just finishing the third kitty.
It was staring up at her from beneath the water,
screaming silently till the bubbles stopped.
She tossed it to the side and grabbed a fourth.

The mother cat paced back and forth
from the dead pile to the living.
Annie pushed her aside. "Go on!" she said.
"Too many cats. What you want?"

Mike elbowed me as we stood mesmerized,
aghast. "Can we go pick currant berries
by the old barn?" She turned her head askew
and called, a little too loudly, "Da-ye,
Da-ye, boy go pick currant berry by barn.
Boy go pick currant berry by barn?"

On the sixth or seventh kitten, old Albert
appeared in the doorway of the milkhouse.
Had on the same filthy bib overalls
he always had on. He looked us over
through tired yellow eyes that matched
his remaining lower tooth, pointed
a crooked arthritic finger and said,
"Go on! But stay on this side
of the fence. Leave that bull alone.
Last time you got him all riled up!
Took me half the day to catch him."
He disappeared as quickly as he'd appeared.

Annie had all the kittens drowned.
She gave us a sideways smile, said, "Go on!"

We walked down the road to the old barn.
Picked a whole bag.
I glanced back at the cow barn,
saw Annie throw the pail of dead kittens
out the back door onto the manure pile.
The mother cat ran to them. She tried
licking them, one by one, back to life.

We walked home in silence
to collect our pay.

MILTON P. EHRLICH

If Only My Name Had Been Nicholas

I wouldn't have been such a scared kid
if my name had been something—anything,
just not Milton, an alien name,
a yellow star of David.

How could it not catch the eye of those toothless oafs
who hoisted me up in the air in 1936?
My 6-year-old legs fluttered in the air,
wordless—when they demanded
to know: "Are you a Jew?"

My bruised mouth stuttered to utter: "I'm a Greek,"
hoping against hope
I could pass for Christian,
and maybe Greek.
They wore swastika armbands,
forced me to salute Hitler
with a shout of Sieg Heil!

Father wanted to call me Nicholas,
but Mother preferred Mordecai,
after her beloved grandfather.
I could have been a tough kid
with a name like Nick,
maybe even, Nick the Prick,

and might have become a pal
of Tony, Frankie and Luigi,
instead of hanging out
with Hebrew School classmates,
Marvin, Norman and Howard.

Father Doesn't Always Know What's Best

Just when I got comfortable
using our double-seater outhouse,
Father said it was time to move again.

We piled into his new Model A Ford,
and he began to yank at the crank
to turn over the motor—but it wouldn't start.

As he returned to the front seat of the car,
he saw my smudged fingers had lingered
on his windshield. The psoriatic rash
on his face flared flaming red.

Growling like a rabid mongrel,
he lunged for me—calling me a dirty Jew.
The name drove a spike into my heart.

In between sobs, I confronted him
with words that made no sound.
As the only Jew in my class,
all I ever heard was Christ killer!

In later years, I realized how much Father
was trying to pass for "white," working
in a waspy corporation for 36 years.

He identified with the enemy,
like Kapos at Auschwitz and Treblinka.

In *The Bridge on the River Kwai,*
Father could well have played the part
of Alec Guinness—helping the enemy
build their bridge.

Outercourse for the Elderly

When we're still standing,
but standing alone,
loneliness will saturate our souls
like mementoes left on tombstones.
When thunder claps, pick up the stones
and heave them toward a burnt red sky.

When cataract eyes can't see
and clocks have stopped,
keep our eyes shut tight
and mouths wide open.
Allow the birds to fly in
and hide your poems
under a rock.

While waiting to leave your body
at the Hebrew Home for the Aged,
don't be a dunce for once in your life.
Listen to the staff reminding us:
Intimacy can keep us alive.

Ladies and gentlemen who retain
a burning light in their eyes
can now join hands, snuggle up
and cuddle in bed.

They can forget about penetration
and enjoy the pleasures of the flesh.
Endorphins released will help them
feel less alone on the journey ahead.

When a nurse makes her rounds
and hears them giggling in bed,
she will tiptoe out of the room
and quietly shut the door.

How He Lived and How He Loved

He resided in the library
when he wasn't roaming
a supermarket parking lot,
pushing carts back to the store—
the only job he ever had.

He never shaved, cut his hair,
or replaced missing teeth.
He refused to wear a belt—
used a rope around his waist.

He never touched another
human being—lived alone
in a furnished room.

A cadaver, only an incantation
of abracadabra could awaken
his sleeping soul.

But when he recited
the erotic narration
of Molly Bloom's soliloquy
in James Joyce's *Ulysses*—

it was almost like a fervent prayer,
written on a full-length mirror
in Ruby Woo red lipstick.

ZEV SHANKEN

An American Jewish Volunteer Remembers the Six Day War

Kibbutz HaSolelim, Galilee, June 1967

I – *The Sand Box*

Day 1: Dug trenches around the children's village.
Covered chicken coop windows so hens in the light
would think it's day and lay eggs during black outs.

Day 2: Poured concrete with hired Arabs and American volunteers
when not in bomb shelter meeting Americans who had settled here
      years ago.
One woman held a *New Yorker* and asked about Edward Albee's
      new play.

Day 3: Filled sandboxes with dirt we'd stored in sacks on Day 1.
The war was virtually over.
Beat swords into plowshares; poured trench dirt into sandboxes.

Days 4 & 5: Returning soldiers gave impromptu battle reports in
      the dark dining hall.
The acoustics were bad, and the Hebrew colloquial.
I didn't understand most of what was said.

Day 6: In the middle of a report, someone turned on the lights.
Dining hall exploded in cheers. Blackout over,
but we heard low flying jets and felt the earth shake all night.

II – *The American Dream*

Saturday: David, who had settled in Israel years ago with the woman
who had asked about Edward Albee's new play, scolded their daughter
for defending Israel's actions in Quneitra.

"They'd have done the same or worse to us," she said in fluent Israeli
     Hebrew.
Her father protested. *Jewish ethics! Lessons of History!*
His Hebrew sounded like mine, like a teacher at a Hebrew-speaking
     summer camp.
His daughter sneered and left the room. He looked at me with shy
exasperation and said, "Teenagers!"

Sunday: Over the eggplant sorting machine, I asked David what will
     become of
the newly conquered territories. He smiled less shyly than yesterday
     and said,
"We'll form a Greater Israel."

Leonard Cohen

He was too much like us to be held in awe.
He did it better, but only better.
His songs moved us because we could tell how.

Didn't we all know guys in Hebrew school
who discovered sex through Buddhist prayer?
Didn't we all devise ambiguities for folk song nights at the JCC?

He was not the angry little genius who each time we heard
we asked where he came from, surely not Minnesota.
He is not departed or gone.

Ellen

She worried that she smelled bad, told me her brother used to call her
     "Stinky,"
but it was nothing like a bad smell. When I think of her in front of me,
     naked, still alive,
I'm in an ocean of soft nets and beige outdated subway maps. I taste

Good & Plenty,
a trace of tooth decay, very slight, and, before the chemo, pot.

What made me think of her today, almost fifty years later?
Could it be her proof of God: that men enjoy fucking women?
Could it be the medical marijuana I'm considering for my back?

I think it's the David Brooks piece in today's *New York Times*
about Bonhoeffer, Benedict and Gerald R. Ford—
three ways to fight the new president.

Remembering Allen Ginsberg and LBJ, I thought up a fourth,
the William Blake we used to quote like lines from old films:
"The weak in courage is strong in cunning."
"Always be ready to speak your mind, and a base man will avoid you."

R. BREMNER

Regarding an occurrence at Queen of Peace Boys' High School, North Arlington, New Jersey, in the year 1969

faces spill from the bridge in the distance
over frozen water that refuses to flow
a wandering crow thinks better of the dance,
declines to alight on these pillars of snow

you can reminisce in this scene of peace
of times before sin destroyed your goal,
but you'll never get the sumptuous guilt to cease,
nor exonerate you from the crime in your soul

Note: the "occurrence" was an ambush and beating, by a popular and powerful student, of a weak, shy, effeminate student. The "crime" was mine, for not doing anything to stop the beating, being fearful of ostracization by much of the senior class, who stood around watching.

(untitled)

A large frozen moon like a lustrous snowball
illuminates the tangle of twigs in a memory
with a sweet, pure, and honest story
as open and white as that moon,
for madness and despair are innocent enough
when the memory hides a leaf
amid trees in a forest.

(after G.K. Chesterton's "Sign of the Broken Sword")

(untitled)

I think I see the light!

Comin' to me, comin' through me!
Givin' me a second sight!
So shine, shine, shine
> —Cat Stevens, "I Think I See the Light"

Despair drips from the clouds, dribbling into my eyes.
I own him, love him, keep him for mine,
Despair follows my footsteps, tripping over my
feet, falling with me to the chalky sidewalk in
hopes of breaking my hip again, this time hoping to
snap it in permanence and send me into blue funk ball-
fields, where I will forever be his lonely dependent.
But I break his storied spell, meet him on his own
level, with vodka and lime and tales of the new and
old progressions and wins and losses and hits
and misses, lost loves, gained knowledges, sand
dunes and snow banks and more clichés than he knows
how to handle till he throws up his hands in
surrender, and I grab him, we walk hand in hand down
Despair's alley, laughing and chatting about our
books that have failed, and our fabulously fast-draining
finances, and the lost innocence of the 1960s, and
Janice's smile and Christina's eyes and Shari's
breasts and even more till the cows come
home and darkness Greets us with a slow
slap in our faces I realize that Despair has
won again like always and there could
not be any possibility of a better tomorrow as
I catch him chortling slyly and again he begins
to drip from the clouds, dribbling into my eyes.

Brainen 4

A hermit was so thankful that there was no milk today that he wrote a
chronicle of his mamas. His papas and strange young girls left with a
starman who plays Debussy when you are near. When the sun went

---

down on forever afternoon, a small circle of friends took money or a story to Coconut Grove and hung out with some fun and tuneful femmes with a kaleidoscope who had a pulsating dream of where the action is. Bill Baily came home to Georgia cotton pickers who looked so good in '66, when they still had mas que nada. Something tender and sweet went out to lunch with Senor Soul and his loco cascades. The abominable snowman and his sister Kate sought a bowlegged man who could bring them freedom, but all they got was Nigerian highlife so they shouted and took a nap. The crossroads of modernism is what makes the world unforgettable for flat foot Sam who went in a frenzy to New Orleans all by himself.

(This Absurdist poem is built from a playlist of Bob Brainen, a disc jockey at WFMU in Jersey City, New Jersey.)

DENISE LA NEVE

Woman in Seventeenth Century House

My mother and I once visited an elderly woman whose name I have now forgotten. A relic, like the house she lived in, like the worn Carboniferous mountain that rises to the east, like a hidden labyrinth through which the wind billows, or like the water flowing beneath our feet to feed the ancient Gallic spring. Her home is plaqued: *La maison a été construite pendant les années 1600,* and from outside it appears charming and innocent, like everything that is small and unassuming. A warm, smiling face welcomes us. Mother respectfully greets her and offers conversation.

As we enter, we are shuttered. The exterior optimism of greenwashed plaster gives way to dank interior cave-like walls that look as if they could have been formed millennia ago. We stand in a room that is colorless and dark, except for one unsettling spot of bright yellow— emanating not from forsythia or daffodils, or any cheerful vibrancy, but from a hanging plastic strip where flies are stuck dead, dying. Does this woman feel the house's agitation, its troubled fading embers, or is it just a reflection of herself?

Forty years a widow. Flesh on flesh no longer creates hot desires. Dimness enhances her scoliotic posture and slow gait. Do her movements recall any of the gaiety of suitors' pursuits? Do her lips remember how to form a kiss, or do they only pucker at the taste of wrinkled plums? She serves preserves, cookies, *des biscuits.* Did she ever laugh at a kite as it wrapped itself around a fluttering breeze? She smiles sweetly as discussion continues in provincial French. I pick up snippets (*J'ai connu votre mère quand elle a eu …*), phrases (*tout le monde …ça va bien…*), yet context is lost. Did she ever waltz with a lover across a ballroom? Today, she shambles slowly across the kitchen's packed earthen floor.

Will she add this day to her repertoire of memorable events, hit replay as loneliness settles in? Or will her eyes flicker, acknowledging that the house may not stand for much longer, envisioning its destruction and her own? The day wanes, and the soft light diminishes further. Shadows hide in dark corners and whisper, then fall silent. Even the ghosts of the past now dissolve into blackness.

Go-Go Boots in Grand Pa's Garden

sky blue dress
hemmed just above the knee
with white go-go boots,
clothes for vegetable picking.

not like my grandfather's pants
of forest green
or Danish wooden clogs
that he cleaned on every return
(mud chipped off,
exposing a dull shine).

my reflective footwear
highlighted teenage fashion,
but at day's end
the soft wet loam
clung to them as well.

my grandfather smiled
at my working attire,
then showed me
how to pick radishes,
snap off *legumes* from vines,
taste the sweetness of peas.

little was spoken

during this daily ritual.
his English consisted of few words,
my French only slightly better.
the language barrier melted away
with the leafy feel of lettuce,
a last pull on a rooted carrot
or firm tugs that yielded tomatoes.

the woven basket filled,
chores finished,
we walked down earthen stairs
to deposit raw ingredients
for an evening meal.

after removing shoes,
sweaty feet slid
into soft slippers,
and we retreated to the kitchen's warmth,
leaving a young girl's boots
and an old man's clogs
standing side by side.

JENNIFER POTEET

Flame

I don't remember the name of the first boy I kissed
in the year of our nation's bicentennial—
just his sour smell—like firewood,
and that he was available and eager at the July 4th picnic.
Indeed, a faint spark passed between us
as I met the tinder of his lips.
I was at summer camp, and twelve.

That August, Eric Gruber strolled his way
down to me, past a line of pining girls,
white tee-shirt sleeves rolled.
Eric smoked. He was from many towns.
We kissed and caressed
on the assenting grass by the lake
until our lips and hands burned.

And now, October. Some forty years later.
In my backyard, under the elms.
I don't know what happened
to either of those boys, but I'm still
that open-mouthed girl.
Delirious leaves careen;
I listen as the wind picks up.
It whispers. It promises: *Yes*.

Returning Movies to an Ex-Husband

Here I am, on a godless August Sunday,
with the last load:
Westerns, their dried-up labels curled
on plastic spines,
marked in your tiny, efficient script.

Your house is dead
on a joyless street.
How can you stand to live
in this ruined, rented room:
cracked linoleum, rust-stained toilet hissing?

The yellow brocade chair, you boast,
and hold out for me in embroidered gallantry,
was left out on the curb.

I slip into the waiting Honda.
Slow pull away.
Behind the bent, lowered blinds,
you darken, fade,
disappear.

Our New York Trip

after Ring Lardner and Frank O'Hara

What a great, steady gig you've got
if you're a Radio City Rockette!
Sure, they always gotta wax their stems and kick
kick kick with the same fervor
as the gal next to them, at the same height,
and sometimes they've got five performances
in the same day. There's black and yellow
legs now, kicking next to white ones.
Everybody spends their dough to celebrate that elevation.
We wondered: when do the girls get to have lunch?
When the wife and I went, we ate fried chicken on the bus.
These dancers eat on the fly, they say: stuff almonds in their garters,
hide raisins in the pockets of their skirts.
On the avenue, between shows, we saw hustlers peddle
loot between the cabs and the office stiffs,

both rented backs hunched
as jackhammers agitated the pavement.
We witnessed an argument over a sandwich,
followed the crawl of the day's news,
then escaped back inside Radio City's deco dazzle,
—a palace for the people—
to admire, again, their Mighty Wurlitzer.

ALICE TWOMBLY

Phonograph/Photograph

You make me think of the rituals
of cleaning records so carefully
that no fingerprint or dust could mar their pristine surfaces,
or produce a scratch that would forever ruin Joan Baez's crystalline
voice.

Remember how we used to watch
just how gently and precisely
the perfectly balanced arm of the Dual turntable
would descend to kiss the surface of the LP
with the shyest but most erotic of caresses

and, then, there would be perfection.

Unveiling: for Isidor Jacobs

I

March wind
April rain
A Sunday morn

Grass struggling
Through cracked flat stones
Here lies my father

Dressed in his last suit
An Arrow shirt
A tie that hugs his shrunken bones

II

The brothers gather near the ruptured soil
Blinking in the wind

Somewhere well beneath their eyes
Their silent bond of loving lies

The rain makes mud holes
Of the new dug graves

III

The Kaddush read
The prayer intoned

I carve these words
In skin, on bone

"My father is
A piece of stone"

MARIAN CALABRO

Edvard Munch's Madonna

He paints a Madonna, as all artists must.
But the woman looks troubled, gray. Closed eyes.
Half dressed. A midnight blue sky fades to black.
Black swirls around her. Indefinite breasts,
Not full enough to suckle anyone,
So Munch's Madonna hasn't earned her name.
And the baby in question is barely
An embryo, stuffed into the corner
Of the frame, its eyes open, large, wary,
Begging *please don't birth me, you're not ready.*
Munch paints the frame, too, as artists shouldn't.
Nine sad spermatozoa with no eggs
In sight. No surprise, as this Madonna
Has no details from the waist down.

Why I Am Like New Jersey

North and south halves different:
One facing the Manhattan skyline,
the other mired in sameness,
the tea-still water of the Pine Barrens.

Lots of potholes and too many red lights
threaten to slow the flow of creativity,
but I barrel through the amber:
nothing like a deadline in any medium.

A high point that is not very high,
prosaically named High Point.
Lows, accompanied by mosquitoes
and the occasional lightning bug.

Home rule? For sure.
My mind has at least 595 municipalities
fighting for their fair share,
each with its own police chief.

Spaghetti and meatballs
as good as anyone's.
I'm talking to you,
country shaped like a boot.

CATHARINE CAVALLONE

Autocorrect

I want to bitch-slap you,
Autocorrect.
You got no business fixin' me—
Yeah, I don't feel like a 'g' today,
you got a problem with that?
If you sat down next to me
on the subway, I would just
fuck you up.
You and your white-ass
grammar rules,
changin' what I say every day—
and no, not 'elegant gays'—
every day.
What if I called you *automobile*
or *autoerotic* or
autocrat?
You wouldn't like that very much,
would you.
You think you're one step ahead of me,
but you ain't.
Because your '*suggestion*' is
NOT what I meant to say, bitch.
I text my husband to buy *bread*
and you 'suggest' that he buy *head*!
What kinda monster are you?!
I write my friend I'll be late
and you tell her I'll be "latte"!
How often does the word "latte"
come up in texting? Unless you're some
faggoty-ass barrista in *Seattle*?
Granted—you're good with apostrophes,
but even if you weren't,

my peeps would still be able to
make out what I say.
But they do NOT understand
'elegant gays', bitch.
You're just tryin' to mess me up,
cuz you're a machine and I'm a lady.
You're jealous!
You think you're HAL,
you think you're AI, but you ain't.
You're just a feature,
tryin' to call attention to yourself.
"Look at me, look what I can do!"
Well, let me tell you somethin', honey…
I can breathe, talk, shit, walk *and* spell,
and you ain't never…EVER…
gonna replace me.

PAUL NASH

Of Bread and Man

The boundless universe in a jar,
        so soft, so spreadable.
Life was a scab on his finger that itched;
he scratched and bled slowly to death . . .

A distant methodical thundering,
source unseen, approaching.
A computerized storm?
No, a shadow,
        a greater shadow engulfing his own.

Peanut-butter screams, jellied agony!
On the sidewalk, his remains sizzled in the sun,
then solidified
        in perfect likeness to the scab.

An immense form looked back and grinned;
the ant wiped its foot and walked on,
searching for others.

Terrene

We live inside ourselves . . .
our bacteria call the shots.

BARBARA R. WILLIAMS-HUBBARD

For the Love of Fireflies

Twinkles in the dark
hark the night forward
into moonlight
and the soft sounds
of crickets
lulling body and mind
into a place of rest.
These little lights are guests
within my journey.
They guide.
My eyes follow
the here and there
of their everywhere
until one lights
upon my knee
to share the quiet
and agree
we've each a right
to live,
to shine our lights,
to twinkle
and to be.

The Dish

It's a diamond—
shaped over 100 years ago
to grace a dining room table
with tempting treats
and to lace family gatherings
with smiles and sweets.

It's a royal dish—
rose-colored glass adorned
with feet of gold
and a gold-patterned lid
with a pyramid knob
facing East and West, North and South.
In times past, one section
held the Dutch Hoppes—
coffee-flavored hard caramels
that we sucked until
the last bit of caramel
melted deliciously in our mouths.
The other section held
small bites of licorice
we were convinced we couldn't do without.
When we were small,
we'd hide under the table
and try to sneak a treat or two.
Sometimes, we were caught,
and sometimes we were shooed.
It is a diamond,
my memory of past years
of a grandfather's hand
lifting the lid,
and a grandmother's smile
nodding to his bid,
as we, the little ones,
stood and grinned expectantly
from ear to ear.

JAMES B. NICOLA

wind chimes

Any
   any poem   about

about   wind chimes
    would have to look a lot
a lot
      lot
      lot
      lot

like   this.

GIA GRILLO

From Iggy Pop in Reply to a 20 Page Fan Letter

Dear L

i read the whole fucking thing, dear.

to see you   black dress   white socks

to see you   take a deep breath   and do whatever you must

to survive   find something to be   that you can love.

YOU: a bright fucking chick w/ a big heart w/ a happy spirit.

i was very miserable

fighting hard on my 21st b'day

people booed

in someone else's house

I was scared.

'perforation problems' by the way

means the holes that always exist

in the story we make of our lives.

hang on, my love, grow big and strong

And strong

that's you L

That's you

iggy

Hidden Away

The drawer is stuck.
      A pair of scissors jammed forcefully inside is
      keeping Schrödinger secrets.
Everything I need is in there
                and isn't.

Misunderstood

Ryan was right.
      Harry Dean Stanton is a perfect animal
      with Bukowski on his lips.
I could be a perfect animal, too.

D. M. DUTCHER

Specifications

A tiny black spider climbed up
my white wall looking like this period .
with a swirl of miniature commas attached,
all pumping with the exquisite coordination
that nature hardwires into those to whom
it gives such minimal brains.
Climbed, that is, till the eyes in the back
of its head saw my eyes peering back at it,
then headed straight for the corner.
How does it know to do that'?
How does it know it's harder to get at,
to peck at, to become food while hidden there?
And what is this eye-identifying ability?
Sitting six feet away when I saw it,
it saw me seeing it, and it was too small
to tell if it even had eyes. So there's actually
a gene that programs this speck to recognize
eyeballs from afar, having never seen eyeballs before,
go into defensive mode, and seek out corners because
it's safe there? Then I thought maybe it's we,
with our sense of dominance over nature,
who have the limited brains, and as I reached
for pencil and paper, I took my eyes off it,
and off it went.

RIA TORRICELLI

"missed"

the floor is clean where your furniture was
I run my finger in and out of the dust
erase the chalk outline
that marks the death of us
I don't dream of you anymore
even if I plant the seed
reality is the barren land
where even hope won't root
I lie and say I wish you luck
and happiness and peace and love
when all I really want
is our combined misery
so I can lean on you
and you'll let me see you weep
instead I tuck in on myself
my knees soaked through with tears
and listen to the echo song
and wait for you to come back home
and pray for you to come back home
and wonder how I'll still go on
when there's no doubt that you've moved on
that you are gone
you are gone

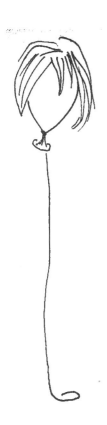

"emotional dieting"

aching for mercy
the pressure builds
an overfilled balloon
she runs her fingers through her own hair
and pretends it's someone else
no one ever said it would be easy
this solitary life
dinner standing at the sink
cold sheets on half of the bed
and the quiet

If she moves from room to room
and no one is there to see it
does she really exist?
this is what she wants
what she needs
it is her unspoken mantra
her self-induced confinement
a way to reconnect
with everything inside
to want again
and feel again
for the right reasons
if only she could stifle
the desire to be touched
understood
needed
adored
the rest would come easy
instead she is hungry
choking down her freedom
and craving something more

JIM KLEIN

Fazia's Wedding

After Reading Williams' "The Pink Church,"
I am unmanned to go on about Fazia's wedding
at which we arrived late
because we rode the brakes all the way
to The Little Wedding Chapel,
the turnpike bumper to bumper
fixing winter disrepair.
(I signed as a witness
having only seen the picture-taking.)
But The Little Wedding Chapel
was nothing, this union
of Hindu and Muslim,
nay Pentecostals, (and immigrants)—
childhood sweethearts separated
by life to wed middle-aged, with four kids,
in a new family already seven years underway,
God damn The Little Wedding Chapel!
I say the reception was the ceremony,
secular for sure with an MC
as gross as Donald Trump,
but he read Fazia's testament,
a true rendering
of the lines of force
that had brought them
all together in this
critical mass because
she was that honest,
and fulsome—the six
making testament, and true—
theirs was a holy family,
and pure, having lived in
sin these seven years,

if there is such a thing,
the six together, lives
running as rich as
the standing rib roast

Ted Williams

To actually
see the ball
on the bat
as he hit

was
Ted Williams'
lasting ambition.

I'd like to see
the poem
mean,

      see
sense like
wind on water,

meaning like
the crack of a whip

rhetoric gentle
as a wisp of hair,

jump rope
rhythm.

It would be
good to fuse

word and
meaning,

     maybe
bring the poem
to a stop

and walk
behind it,

or get up
on a ladder
to buff and
lubricate it.

I wish for
stop actions
to see how
the damn thing
works,

I'd like to
become
the poem,
and have
the poem
become
me,

to have
its breath
be mine,
and its soul
a moment
in mine.

Nail Clipping

We're head to toe,
naked, crosswise,
like scars on the bed,
clipping my toenails—
it's not romantic, or even
necessary, but the bath
softens the big toenail—
and she gets busy
with her task bending
close to my feet under
the light, a woman
attending to her
husband's feet,
in delight, as the
work goes evenly,
collecting the soft
nail parts, handing
the largest one to me,
and I lie ecstatic, her
hard nates in my
palm, varying
smoothnesses
in delightful phases,
only occasionally
glimpsing into the
cove her legs make,
and along the ridge
of her scarcely
moving back to
the studying head
bent to its work.

Cezanne Said
a Painter
Needs Balls

He used just
enough blue
to suggest air,
to make it seem
you could walk
behind his subjects,
and not have them
look pasted on
the canvas.

Saturday, I painted
to *Double Fantasy*.
I've always thought
John was the one
with balls, but
this time I was
moved by Yoko's
singing, especially
when she was
masturbating

and I squeezed
a tube of white
violently all over
as long as she
lasted

The Thumb Cork

"I kissed her while she pissed."
  —"Turkey in the Straw," WCW

Slept soundly until
I got up with a loud fart
at 6,

  got back into bed
and encountered
her ire.

  Right in my face!

  I wasn't that close

 . . .

  I forgive you, I sd

  You're not Jesus

  Well, I'm a follower, at least
I'm not a Muslim

She goes go the bathroom
and tries to pay me back,
but farts sideways.

  I'm not a Muslim
And my parents aren't either

  But you don't forgive much

She leaves and comes back

threatening me with a belt.

I've been beaten with a belt

Don't tell me about beatings
I was knocked into a pie safe once
and had my eye closed for a week
and I slept five hours

What were your parents then?

I've been beaten with fists
on the top of my head

.   .   .

She starts laughing loudly,
remembers little kids talking about
          hearing their parents fart.

One kid had never heard his mother fart.

          Someone asked
Did she have a thumb cork?

She had never heard that,
but she knew what a *thumb cork* was!

(laughing, laughing, laughing).

She decides she is falling in love

with Pippa, (almost as much
as Pretty Boy) and has to get up.

> *Do you want both fans on?*

> *Yes*

> *It's a waste of electricity*

> *I get my electricity from the sun*

> *Still, you shouldn't waste it*

> *The SUN!*

JOEL ALLEGRETTI

Pig Child

I. His Birth

He by the grace of God entered the world at two forty-five on a
midwinter morning.

Mother of Pig-Child-to-Come lay on the bed like a Thanksgiving
turkey blessed with the gift of speech & Grandma's kisses sugared her
brow & Emma the midwife sang "*What wondrous love is this, O my
soul, O my soul?*" Father-in-Waiting dozed in the corner & Nimrod the
retriever sniffed at every crack & orifice till Grandma's hand came
down on his haunches—a five-finger electrical storm.

When the baby arrived bulbous & greasy & cranberry-blood-clotted
Emma cried "Get thee behind me, Satan" it wasn't her doing she was
just the midwife & Mother wept a fountain of Christ's blood &
Grandma cast a carrion-eater's eye on her son-in-law & proclaimed
loud enough for the neighbors' ears, "Marry a pig & a pig begets a
pig."

II. Spiteful Girls' Double-Dutch Schoolyard Rhyme

Lady bug, lady bug
Hop frog, toad
Who could that be
Coming down the road?

        Oak tree, maple tree
        Rosebud, twig
        Could be a boy
        But it looks like a pig.

> Butterfly, dragonfly
> Carolina wife
> Careful, Pig Child
> Butcher got a knife.

III. Mother of Pig Child, or Meditations for the Seven Days
     of the Week

Mary Jean Leeds might have been the first female astronaut—
or at least homecoming queen—if:

Day One

She wore patent-leather shoes.

Day Two

She hadn't married below the station of a deer tick.

Day Three

Rosebushes grew in the Pine Barrens.

Day Four

Eve had turned a deaf ear to the serpent.

Day Five

Rain didn't fall in Burlington County.

Day Six

She didn't have to slit the seat of her son's pants to
make room for an unorthodox body part.

Day Seven

God hadn't nodded off.

IV. And the Lord Inquired

The livestock judges at the county fair judged themselves clever when they awarded Pig Child's parents a blue ribbon for their boy.

*

THE LORD

When is a badge of honor not a badge of honor?

CHERUBIM

When only the moon can hear you sigh.

V. Spiteful Girls' Double-Dutch Schoolyard Rhyme

Pig Child, Pig Child,
Sitting in a tree,
Looking at his mama
Loving Trashman Lee.

Pig Child, Pig Child,
Why you got a tail?
Got to pick the lock
& get my daddy out of jail.

Pig Child, Pig Child,
Where your mama go?
Mama's lying fast asleep
Underneath the snow.

VI. Pig Child's Discourse on the Wonders of Astronomy

The night of the meteor shower.
Pig Child marveled,
"Why, Mama, even the stars have tails!"

VII. Moon Gone Down

whole & yellow
sky-born custard tart

gone down dawn's
wide slippery throat

half dipped in the horizon
could be God's droopy eyelid

day's a kitchen door
swinging slowly open

in our little world our sleep
is our prayer for peace

Semen Elegy

To J.E.A.

You, long housed in a crypt, relic
in a reliquary, subsist on my Now,

more present than in your years of
skin + bone + voice + judgment,

---

as indelible as a dress shirt and ascot,
your fingerprints marking my solvency.

Your profound teaching, however,
wasn't the achievements of your life,

but the petulance of your leaving:
how you snarled at the diminishing

sand to the beat of the morphine drip;
how you stood your ground while flat

on your back, straining to smack Death's
exacting hand; and how you clawed like

a jungle cat and spat in the leveler's eye
seconds before his greedy fingers glee-

fully pinched your stubborn lips
shut.

BOB MURKEN

Brooklyn Bridge

And we have seen night lifted in thine arms.
                    —"To Brooklyn Bridge," Hart Crane

Great cathedral of a bridge,
you point your Gothic arches skyward
cut in blocks of weathered stone,
strung with cables densely webbed

for strumming by the ocean winds
that hum for us in solemn plainchant
what this city and its harbor

had to sing about
a hundred years ago.

Demolition

The hundred-year-old wall of brick
did not resist the wrecking ball.

Instead, it folded, toppled, vanished,
cascading mortar and debris.

Caught unprepared, my house just lost,
for all to see, its privacy,

bared room-sized squares—red, white and green—
and a wooden staircase standing free.

Such unsuspected symmetry,
the geograph of a former world!

—The special space I took for granted
  was just this much and nothing more?

I suspect what I just saw
might be a kind of metaphor.
If it's trying to tell me something . . .
I'm not sure I want to listen.

THE RUTHERFORD RED WHEELBARROW

Diner Waitress

"My name is Tammy, and I'll be
your server for tonight.
A twist of fresh-ground pepper?
Some grated parmesan, perhaps?"

Look,
if hunger really sharpens wits,
we well-fed folk can learn from her.
She works all day, can raise two kids,
still stay attractive, neat and perky,
live on what she makes on tips,
still take a night course in accounting.

Her memory amazes me.
"Mango salsa? Demi-glaze?
Balsamic vinegar reduction?
Bordeaux Chicken Casoulet,
or Meat Loaf a la Tuscany?"
What exactly are those things?
She knows, is willing to explain.

And would the chef omit the spice?
Keep sauce separate on the side?—
And when do you get off from work?

"Of course.
Of course.
None of your business.

—Some dessert, perhaps?"

ALFRED ENCARNACION

Hong Kong, Mississippi

You don't sound like where you from,
I know—you from Hong Kong, Mississippi!
                              —Bo Diddley

You won't get there by map,
no matter how long you pore
over one. Consult any road
atlas, as if an astrological
chart, you'll still draw up a blank.
There are no demographics
offered by the U.S. Census, no
State guide books to reference
your journey into the delta.
Word of mouth would be best,
but who can trust language?
Besides, local residents all keep
a tight lip; they sound
and look like typical inhabitants.
Who would guess they're not?
Only the truly conflicted,
for whom incongruity wounds,
will sense the powers they wield,
the mysticism that shrouds
their down-home Shangri-La.
Only pure desperation leads
to this place of healing,
where the image in your mind
matches the face in your mirror,
and the shame-dragon's driven
at long last away. The desperate
will know what turn to make
at the crossroads to nowhere,

the one back road to follow
out to the bridge that collapsed
years ago in a loud cloud of dust,
yet still can be crossed if paid
its full toll of grief. Few will
arrive at that town lost
in the fields of cotton,
its temples and pagodas
shimmering in the sun
like a *Taoist* painting where
Buddha transcends the blues,
watching a white butterfly rise
and enter the moment.

The Diving Bell, Atlantic City, 1963

We're locked inside
a crowded metal
shell hunkered
deep in the gray
Atlantic. I hunger
for the exotic, expect
the silver blur
of sharks with ivory
teeth. No dice.
We see no fish,
no plants in
this dark bowl
of saltwater. At last
the bell begins
its rise toward
the floating
light...

30 years later

we surface
in a hushed white
room; nurses like
angelfish stream
past the bed
where you
struggle behind
a respirator
mask. I listen
to your breaths
ebb farther
apart, imagine
a bell—stranger
than the one
we once rode—
drawing the sick
up out of their
deathbeds

to enter

its chamber
of amber sea-
light. Drowned
in fathoms of cold
sunken gloom,
a shadow flickers,
a sleek fin circles
the room.

DANIEL P. QUINN

Quintillion's (net) 4 Newark

Standing
near
Broad St.
station,
alone,

I am
in bloom

as the
King
of my
Transit
Plaza.

In
Jersey
we
never say
Piazza

even
when
I
used to
hear
about
Nevarca
from
my
Grandfather
Tree.

I
have
neighbors
and grass
at my feet.

Now,
they are
almost
gone.

But
I am
still
here.

My trunk
strives
to make
an impression.

My rings
document
my life.

My trunk
cracks open
the stifling
black top
that used
to
engulf me.

I
am

a
survivor.

I live in Newark.

Across the street,
I await for
more destruction.

The few trees
that surround
my old friend
Bears Stadium
are now
doomed.

I provide
shade
in the summer.

I have grown
these last
20 or 30 years
to showcase
my stressful
life
in spite
of my
almost vacant
plaza.

Some times,
a few times,
people
sit
around me.

There
once was
pizazz
in Newark
at
Bears
then Riverside
Stadium
as
it
sits
forlornly
Struggling
to survive,

Hoping
for another
30 or more
years
of life.

But,
alas,
I am alone,
and have
no progeny.

I
am
a
Tree
in Newark.

I had hope,
when the

engineering
firm
designed
my
NJ Transit
neighborhood.

They planted me.

But,
everything
became
ugly:

the grass,
suffocated
and
died,

Now
all that remains
is
the
blacktop.

The Circus
was across
the street
a few weeks ago.

The wind blew my
branches,
as I waved,
at the children
going by.

Don't
be
afraid
of
me.

I live in Newark,
as a tree . . .

JOHN DULL

Beneath

In the dump,
Behind the sheet,
Over the protube,
Under the heap—
Something still is creeping there.

It's something deep in canyons steep,
In seeping garbage
Makes its keep,
And someday, somehow we will reap
The fruit of seeds
And deeds that simmer
Deep beneath.

If I Was an Hermaphrodite

 If I was an hermaphrodite
Would you quite know how to take me?
Would you try to make me into you?
Declare which organs I could use?
Would you tell me how it is I feel?

                ***

Who are we?—the hypocrites
Who sit and ponder every day,
Telling others how to shit
And authorizing all the ways
We deal with love.

***

If I was an hermaphrodite
Would you quite know how to take me?
Would you try to make me into you?
Declare which organs I could use?
Would you tell me how it is I feel?

Lego Spirits

The Lego spirits threw down some blocks
And clicked them into a nice tall box . . .
Then two, and three, and even four,
And over decades thousands more.

In somber session, they deemed it "pretty,"
And bade we name it New York City.

DAN SAXON

Words

I love the blank page
Nothing
But thoughts
To fill it up
Like fuel for a car
Food for energy,
So here I am
In control,
Playing with words
Never before sequenced
By a living human being
On this date
As far as I know
Creating unique
Memorabilia
For you
To contemplate,
Extol,
Cast aside…

Paradise

Writing is fun
If it wasn't
I wouldn't be here
I would be digging my grave
gazing at the stars
waiting for a driverless car
to take me to paradise.
I can imagine
a better world

I will never get to.
We have just about seen
it all or thought we did, so
what will happen next
we can never know
except something will, so
we should know the exit signs,
the escape routes,
in case paradise is not an option, and
all we can do is find our way
through darkness,
towards a more hopeful
welcoming light…

Procedure Notes

Two more eight-ounce glasses of water, and
I have completed my preparation for
a colonoscopy,
my second in five years.
This pristine three-foot section
should be ready for probing for
twenty minutes to one-half hour with
a tube about one-half inches in diameter,
flashlight and scissors attached
to sever any polyps, intrusions, etc.
It has not been that bad,
chicken broth, white grape juice,
Jello
Just another procedure for
preventive medicine to
catch the culprit early and hopefully
prevent one's demise before
it's too late…

GORDON GILBERT

Winter Road to Ithaca

Proceeding north, I drive down 79 west
With a two-o'clock southwest sun already low,
Heavy on my left shoulder,
Throwing occasional shadows
Across this two-lane highway.

Ahead, the road drops down into a hollow;
On the left, the hillside cut away;
Above, ridge-topped, a file of beech
Cast tall, straight shadows
Across the salt-dusted asphalt.

And, as I run this gauntlet of tree shadows,
I am again a boy with stick in hand
Running along the neighbor's picket fence,
Exuberant, empowered by the simple rhythm
Of the note I strike, a childhood song.

AMY BARONE

Visions

The night of the Steven Wilson concert,
I awoke every twenty minutes haunted
by visions—a man's face locked in a frame.

Was it the prog rock singer of Porcupine Tree fame?
I had joined zealots of his 'poetry of melancholy'
at the sold-out Beacon Theatre gig. They were

heading to Chicago for the next show. A neophyte,
I listened and watched his performance in awe.
Massive video art as backdrop with everyday

London scenes starring a sultry brunette, the desert,
shades of yellow and purple. Singer Ninet Tayeb
joined him onstage as he drank tea to combat a cold.

The night ended with their duo of Bowie's "Space Oddity"
as a striking headshot of the late prophet lit up the stage.

Power in a Thumb

When phones were immobile
and laptops futuristic,
we possessed little money,
but owned freedom.

Minutes overflowed.
Boredom afflicted us endlessly;
we embraced it.

Planning was for bores.

When we got too big for our bikes,
in our hip huggers, midriff tops and sneakers,

we sought danger.
All we had to do
was wear a sultry scowl

and flash a thumb.
We trusted strangers to take us
anywhere we wanted to go.

MELENE KUBAT

Dark Matter

I never knew ashes
could feel so darn heavy
until the day,
fifteen years later,
I packed yours on my back,
to scatter them
close to the lake
where we listened for frogs
in the forest we hiked
before our lives shattered.

Was it the ashes,
or grief
in remission,
now fast reemerging
as dust on a surface
nearly as soon
as it's polished.

I suspect you knew
where you were going,
perhaps having crossed
some invisible border
or finding a parallel life
during months in a coma
years before I had known you—
but to me it is so much dark matter,
and I wish you could show me.

The Sacred and the Profane (Poetry Reading at Storm King)

After the reading,
while we were clapping,
I rose to leave, reluctantly.
A boy uninterested
in poetry
was waiting for me
elsewhere in the sculpture park.

I wanted to say
how astonished I was
by a poem that you read,
work-in-progress you said.
I liked that you paused
between verses
to take off your shoes,
and that you revised
several lines of your
poems as you read.
No poem was ever
really finished,
you said.

I wanted to stay,
perhaps have you sign
one of your books
that I already owned,
but mostly I wanted
the lines of your poem
to take root in my head,
spring some shoots of its own,
for I knew all would be decomposed
by the time I got home
and surrendered
to daily routine.

LEILANI McINERNEY

The Pink Dress

My mother died when I was 5.
  I saw her. Still.
    Very still. Quiet.
    Not breathing.

She was beautiful.
  Laid out in a pink dress.
    A crisp pink dress.

I kept waiting for her to move.
  To open one eye. To wink at me.
    Knowingly.

But she didn't.
  I waited.
    And waited.

Then when we were alone, all alone
  Carefully I lifted up her right arm
    And let it drop.

There was this sound
  A sound I remember to this day
    Right now I hear it.

      Wait.

I wasn't 5.

  I was 40!

  It felt as though I was 5 again.

Late in Life

I've become a mother
    Late in life
To a man who used to
    Call me wife.

It's different now
    The things I do
It's as if, dear one,
    You're no longer you.

GAIL KING

The Night Has Many Hours

Encompassing,
fleeting,
stretching sublimely till morning,
piling up on itself.
Only to start pressing down again.
Counting backwards slowly, deliberately,
the night exhausts itself.

Faces

Faces
now old with wrinkles
are alien-looking.
Their faces jaggle my mind.

Their faces jaggle my mind.
Their staring eyes
pierce my conscience.

Why are these faces familiar?
I think I know them from somewhere.
World stage?
No.
Concert stage?
No.
Center stage?
No.
My mental stage?
Yes! That's it!
It is my disguises,
my impersonations.

Now I remember
it is only me.

My Father's Steps

Not light
like Barishnikov's.
Not heavy
like the Jack-in-the-Beanstalk giant.
Not sliding
like a wooden war veteran's leg.
But cur ploppy, cur ploppy.
My sister and I would laugh,
make up songs to fit his foot fall beats
as we three ambled down the street.
We are the a capella minstrels of Windsor Road.

NICOLE ZACH

Sex Law

I don't need no pimp
Nor chief of police
To tell me when to love
Orders in vain
Coming from the pain…
In the ass system
One says no sex
The other sex slave
Either way we run
Because…
"We believe in a land of love"
Which doesn't come cheap
As all good things in life
We pray and the predictions
Gives us strength and hope
And we defy the cops and the mafia
Only to prevail and enjoy life
Because…
There is more to sex law than a man
There is a woman
Who knows the little boy
And his threats
This woman has a voice
And possesses red
And with it she wakes the dead

Sick

Farting
Dreaming of nightmares
Talking to myself
A busted kidney with a tumor hanging off it
Inhaling another cigarette
Hearing voices
Knowing there is no help…
In an A typical anti-psychotic
Prescribed by the Doctor who
Tries to encourage but can't understand
Or is it me who doesn't understand…ME?
Having another drink
Garbage sitting in my lap
Trying to convince me
Murder is key
Praying to the 10 Commandments
It is Jesus who saves
Not the curse of the dumb
My nature as a metaphor
With an open heart
·An open mind
Body is ailing
And doing time
Cops are jealous
And abuse sex…
Harassment overdone
With the aid of the state
Their power plays…
Screaming War

prose

PAMELA HUGHES

In the Meadowlands

Architectural innuendo. All the upward thrust. The steel tips of Manhattan stand on the Eastern horizon. The Empire State building appears to be seeding a cumulus cloud, while the marshes below are uterine in what can grow and develop in the briny waters.

At first it's quiet here. The car engine is off. As I wait near the mudflats between a hill of phragmite reeds that have grown over garbage, I'm throwing furtive glances in the rear view mirror hoping that the passengers in the few passing cars won't see me muttering my lover's entreaties. Except for me and the two sandpipers that are pecking at a puddle of rainwater on the rutted asphalt road next to the marshes, no one is around. I glance in the rear view mirror again. My husband might not like it that I've written a poem to another, that in it I mentioned the word marry, that I wanted to marry again, or worse, have two marriages, that I wrote a poem, then a book of poems for this other, when he only got four or five poems.

I look out of the windshield and wait. The nuances of sound reach my inner ear. The wind sifting through the phragmites sounds like sand pouring from a bucket onto the beach. I hear the trill of a red-winged blackbird. From the upper branches of the poplar tree standing in front of the landfill overgrown with phragmites, three leaves are waving at me. Friendly, as if those few leaves welcome what care I have for the poplars, the phragmites, the flocks of migratory birds winging their way through or stopping on the mudflats, while the hundreds of other leaves ignore me for what random waste I create or have created by the very act of being human—

exhaust from my Camry, every chemical that came off my squeaky clean girlhood and slipped into the groundwater; the garbage *under* that phragmite hill that is probably mine or some of my family's: our four spent refrigerators, a TV or two, a pair of prescription aviator frames, baby bottles, other assorted glass, reams of paper, toys, old defluffed stuffed animals, a Scooby Doo (don't), the pair of red Keds high tops (but not the boxes and boxes of bloody OB tampons—they went into the waterways), all the bones laid bare of the many meats my mother cooked for us in our pink aluminum-sided rectangle set near the edge of the meadows, and that small (in the gargantuan face of disposable), ragged, though very rugged, pile of my white cloth baby diapers from before I could stand up for the meadows.

Layers of words like a landfill.

The Lenape Indians made no tracks through the indigenous grasses, the salt meadow cord grass and *spartina patens*, or around the forest of Atlantic white cedar and old school pools of fresh water that lay between Lyndhurst and the Hudson River. This, before the Dutch came and built dykes that let in too much salt water, stopped the natural flow of the tides and killed off the forest of cedars. 265 kinds of birds live in these wetlands all year round.

Atlantic Flyway. Atomic number 80. Besides birds, there is a lot of this element in the meadowlands. Mercury. Quicksilver cancer amid the nourishing creeks and brackish waterways, the mix of fresh and salt water. If you swam in Berry's Creek north of Dekorte Park, you might grow mad with joy. Some of the highest amounts of mercury in freshwater sediments in the world can be found in a section of Berry's Creek near the Meadowlands Sports Complex. All around, the phragmites have erected a mighty wall so strong you would need a machete to cut through; the roots spread by way of rhizomes and stolons. Some marsh plants can chelate (which is Latin for "to claw") heavy metals like mercury by way of phytochelatins, so you could say that if the Amazon is the lungs of the earth, than the meadowlands are the liver.

But no amount of phytochelatins can clean up a mall. A mega mall. On top of a meadow. Like having some of the most mercury in the world, New Jersey also holds the dubious honor of "having the most shopping malls in one area in the world, with seven malls in a 25 square-mile radius" (50States.com). In East Rutherford, the Xanadu Mall (recently renamed the American Dream Mall) and its indoor ski slope, wave pool, and Egyptian-themed movie theatre mart is stalled on the northern horizon. The riotous colors of the structure's multilayered architectural boxes (now blue and white) surrounded by golden-tasseled phragmites remind me of a Gauguin painting gone wrong combined with an Albrecht Durer landscape.

Two miles away (and two months earlier) as we walked on the boardwalk over the marshes, we stopped to try to figure out what the oval thing was lying a way off in the brackish water. My friend Linda joked, more a truth held in jest, "Is it a turtle or a tire?" As she tilted her head to the side and peered harder, we could hear the metallic whir and clatter of cars and tractor trailers speeding on the Turnpike about a mile to our east. "Tire or turtle?" The Meadowlands, like New Jersey itself, is a juxtaposition of beauty and ugliness, the fecund face of mother earth with father commerce on top or working her from behind.

Suddenly my car has become a bird blind. A great blue heron swoops low over the hood of my Camry like one of the silver planes landing on the tarmac at the nearby Newark Airport. I gawk wide-eyed at its feathered underbelly. While trying not to lose sight of it, I bump my forehead against the windshield. Born in the blocky suburbs, neither a naturalist nor an environmentalist, the sight of wild animals still surprises me. Like the morning I spotted a red fox kit just off the path in Dekorte Park. In the rush to turn on my digital camera, I juggled it clumsily between two hands and ended up dropping it. The pumpkin-orange fox sniffed a fallen tree trunk at the edge of a stand of oak trees, then started to tumble and play. To its playful pokey pup, I became the playful pokey human. I threw myself down on the path in an ungainly sprawl and laughed at the fox's sportive spell of leaping, how it upended itself in one jump, how a leaf was as intriguing to it as it was to me. When I thought it might leave, I scooped the camera off the ground and snapped a photo. In the picture, which was a bit blurry, the fox had just gotten up and was standing on newly elongated legs that stretched babyhood to the limit. It gazed at me, fixedly, unfazed by my presence, happy after its bout of adolescent playfulness.

Less playful now, I roll down the car window and continue to mouth words of support. A lover's prayer. To the south, past the tall electrical towers stretching east toward Jersey City, I see the mountainous closed landfills of Kearny, but not the maze of industrial plants interspersed beyond them. The Meadowlands is host to both the factory, and the olfactory. Like a beer-drinking boyfriend, occasionally the meadows burps and the methane deep from the landfills rises up like a half-digested ale or a gassy bean dip, with an intimation of ocean, a partly spoiled seafood quesadilla, and wafts around the surrounding towns: Lyndhurst, Rutherford, Secaucus, North Arlington, to name a few, then across the Hudson to Manhattan. *The New York Post* would proclaim, "N.J.'S P.U. RIPENS APPLE." NYC creates 32,000 tons of waste a day and, since its Fresh Kills landfill closed in 2002, exports its stink elsewhere.

It was big news when developer Encap Golf Holding was fined $1.054 million when its employees opened a valve on a Kingsland landfill in Lyndhurst and let methane gas shoot into the air unimpeded for two weeks. Encap's "remediation" of the Meadowlands' brownfields was a bad marriage from the start. One that led to physical abuse of the bride. Jeff Tittel, of the NJ Sierra Club, called the fill Encap used, a "toxic wedding cake." Instead of the original fill made of virgin clay that was supposed to cap the landfills, New Jersey officials and the DEP allowed some two and a half million cubic feet of PCB-contaminated construction debris, asbestos-tainted rock, sewage sludge, and PCB/benzene dredge from New York Harbor and surrounding New Jersey waterways to be trucked in and dumped on the landfill. The usual concessions to commerce had been made. The "Miracle in the Meadowlands," as the project was called, was that clean fill was ever mentioned in the first place.

One spring day at the foot of the Meadowlands Encap site in Lyndhurst, as my four-year-old daughter was coloring a green tree and a pink butterfly, scary men in white astronaut suits showed up breathing through strange masks. After some teachers complained of Encap's horrible stench, OSHA inspectors had come to inspect the area downwind of the remediation site.

On the marsh near my car, two white mute swans forage for grass shrimp, copepods or snails in the shallow water of the tidal mudflat, and then stop to pose. Their black Venetian masks reveal selections of face. White foreheads touch and lovely napes curve into a Valentine's Day shape.

Love. My husband would laugh if I told him the truth—that I was in love with a garbage dump, a Brownfield, a meadow in between a marshland, wrapped and warped together on the map of New Jersey. How do I love you? With my nose clamped shut between thumb and forefinger, with my nose pressed to the butterfly bush's fragrant purple cone, with words I wrote on a page that became four lines of a poem: "I'd marry you if I could, / live along the length of your long arms, / in the stems of your broad back, / and irises of your ibises."

The security guard in the silver SUV (working for the NJ Meadowlands Commission) drives past me, a familiar sight parked on the edge of the road. He waves. I wave back. Each day I manifest with light and words like wings to the universe to keep this tract of wrecked beautiful land free of any more Encaps and or other versions of Donald Trump's 20,000 condos. The golf course, of course. (These have already fallen away.) Each morning, while sitting on the side of the road near Saw Mill Creek Trail, I greet the sun, then put the car into gear and drive a circle around the meadows from Disposal Road up the steep street to the top of Valley Brook Ave. While on a straight edge of the lonely curved road, I take my hands off the wheel for a few moments, jut out the flats of my hands, fingertips splayed, palms downward like a magician or a shaman to feel a thousand phragmite tassels spark with light as I proclaim my womanly power to create instead of kill.

WAYNE L. MILLER

Red Wheelbarrow Poets on the Internet

How did you find out about the Red Wheelbarrow Poets? How do you keep up with its news?

If you live near Rutherford, you might have heard about a reading or the weekly workshop from a friend. Attending our events, you might think that our community is a couple of dozen local poets. It's not.

Our Facebook page has over 360 likes. You will find information on the first-Wednesday reading (who's reading, bio, example poem) at the Williams Center. You will also find announcements for the end-of-the-month Friday music/reading cafe at GainVille. The workshop poem-of-the-week is published (surprise) weekly, as chosen by workshop leader Jim Klein. Occasional announcements of local poetry events are also there, as are photos and videos.

Our Facebook group, *Friends of the Red Wheelbarrow*, has over 150 members of the community. Each member can share announcements, poems, postings, etc.

In addition to being posted on our page and group, the two monthly events are shared on the local groups *The Gauntlet* and *NJ Poetry Readings*. The first-Wednesday reading is also shared on the group *Voices of Poetry*, which is based around Cape Cod but has a national reach, and on the group *Facebook Poetry Society*.

Our Wordpress blog has over 230 subscribers. Postings are similar to our Facebook page. Because of the way Wordpress works, each post is tagged "poetry" and goes to the worldwide community of Wordpress users. We have subscribers to the blog from all over the world. The main page of the blog has links to works of some RWB poets (John Barrale, Milton P. Ehrlich, Mark Fogarty, George De Gregorio, Jim Klein, Janet Kolstein, Frances Lombardi-Grahl, Wayne L. Miller, Zorida Mohammed, Amaranth Pavis, Claudia Serea, John J. Trause, Anton Yakovlev), to some RWB poets' websites (Milton P. Ehrlich, Tom V. Gianni, Jr., Loren Kleinman, Wayne L. Miller, Tony

Puma, Claudia Serea, Don Zirilli), to a couple of essays ("The Rutherford Revival," "'The Opposite of Everything': The Life and Times of *Lunch*"), to Jim Klein's paintings and book (*The Dumb Have the Advantage*), and to descriptions of each of the annual journals. Subscribers can optionally receive email notification of new posts.

Twitter is used for event announcements and the poem-of-the-week. The poem-of-the-week, in addition to being posted on Facebook and the blog, is sent to over 100 subscribers by email.

As you can see, we are much larger than 25 poets who show up in Rutherford once or twice a month. Happy writing!

(Note: all subscriber counts are as of mid-July, 2017.)

QR CODES FOR THE RED WHEELBARROW POETS

Facebook (page)
https://www.facebook.com/RWBPoets

Facebook (friend's group)
https://www.facebook.com/groups/573922469459794/

Blog
https://redwheelbarrowpoets.org/

Twitter
https://twitter.com/RWBPoets

Add your email address for the workshop poem-of-the-week
https://zc1.maillist-manage.com/ua/optin?od=11287eca745936&rd=
1329725d04fb6547&sd=1329725d04fb6541&n=11699e4be688440

ARTHUR RUSSELL

About WCW's Poetics

You might think that WCW had a fixed perspective on poetics. Maybe he did, but if he did it was not simple, ideological or programmatic. He was a proponent of conversational speech, but he was prone to using formalistic and poetically elevated verbiage. He was a proponent of Imagism, so called, but he used argument, and rhetorical figures as much as anyone, and more than most.

Look at the poem "The Red Wheelbarrow." It is often cited as a paradigm of imagism—the barrow, the red, the rain water glaze, the chickens—but it begins with argument, specifically, the expression "So much depends / upon." Not much of an argument, you might say, but it is. The force of the image that comes after it depends on that phrase as much as anything depends on the barrow itself.

To begin, take a look at the word "depends" itself. It has an argumentative, almost conditional aspect; when one thing depends on another they are connected causally, logically or morally as in one thing requiring another, or being a condition precedent to another. "Depends" is also an image because it has the same Latin root as "pendulum" or "pendulous," and it refers to something that hangs. Put that conditional aspect aside for a moment, and see how the poem "hangs down" from that first couplet just as the "so much" "hangs down" from the barrow. One arrow points down and the other arrow points up. And this visual root that is embedded in the diction—the choice of "depends" as the lone verb—animates the whole poem, imagistically as well as conceptually.

To appreciate how forceful the argumentative aspect is, imagine this poem without "So much depends / upon." "[A] red wheel / barrow / glazed with rain / water / beside the white / chickens" is a forgettable imagist poem. "So much depends / upon" imbues the image with immanence. The disproportion between the expectations created by "So much depends / upon" and the quotidian barrow creates a tension that can only be resolved by reconsidering both the barrow and the things the reader might otherwise consider important. That

---

reconsideration, and the swiftness (and irrevocability) with which it occurs, are the magic of the poem.

My point is that one of the poles of this powerful transformation is pure argument, and not imagistic at all. Contrast that to Pound's "In a Station In the Metro," where "The apparition of these faces in a crowd" butts up against "Petals on a wet, black bough," and the force of the poem comes from the mind's metaphoric ability to distill essences from two otherwise disparate objects. It is hard to find any rhetorical content in Pound's poem, unless it comes from the title itself or from the word "apparition." Pound's poem is pure imagism, though he was not an imagist. WCW is not an imagist at all. His poetics is not imagism.

What then is WCW's poetics? It is open-mindedness. Open-mindedness guides his approach, his method, his product and also the effect he seeks to achieve in the reader. That paramount concern abides in the first line of *Paterson*: "Rigor of beauty is the quest. But how will you find beauty when it is locked in the mind past all remonstrance." The emphasis on open-mindedness resides equally throughout the Preface to *Paterson*, with lines like "let / him beware lest he turn to no more than / the writing of stale poems. . . / Minds like beds always made up, / (more stony than a shore). . . ."

Open-mindedness is a virtue that excuses other vices. Look at WCW's elegy for Ford Madox Ford, "To Ford Madox Ford in Heaven." The first thing to notice, before we get to the open-mindedness, is that it is a stale poem. It is verbose, windy and flat. It begins by asking FMF if things are any better in heaven than in Provence (his favorite place). WCW answers: "I don't think so for you made Provence a / heaven by your praise of it / to give a foretaste of what might be / your joy in the present circumstances." The use of the elephantine "for" to mean "because" is the first clue that this poem is in trouble; the line ending with the indefinite article "a" reinforces that impression, and the whole idea of a being as terrestrial as WCW mucking around in "foretastes" of "heaven" makes this poem the stuff of a toast at a wake. The second stanza is as bad as the first.

But the third stanza is somewhat charmed. WCW falls into a conversational dialogue with a see-saw, jagged cadence that starts off with the same mawkish heaven talk, but winds up illuminating FMF's virtues and forgiving his faults. WCW draws up and confronts his unbelieving self, saying he cares not a damn about heaven, except as it might mean cherishing a friend in remembrance, but then he continues:

> Thank God you
> were not delicate, you let the world in
> and lied! damn it you lied grossly
> sometimes. But it was all, I
> see now, a carelessness, the part of a man
> that is homeless here on earth.

The line "Thank God you / were not delicate, you let the world in / and lied! damn it you lied grossly / sometimes" is a wonder of cross currents, a celebration of the rough and ready and of open-mindedness that pivots angrily at the recollection of FMF's equivocation. The final sentence, over three lines, drives towards acceptance of FMF's "carelessness" (a word that settles somewhere ambiguously between *insouciance* and *negligence*) and the recognition that there is a "part of a man that is homeless here on earth." This is good poetry from WCW; it reveals a mind at work, enacting the matter it celebrates and simultaneously placing it in the world. This is an importance part of his poetics.

The Preface to *Paterson* prescribes "open-mindedness"; it also suggests a methodology for poetry that WCW calls "rolling up," a process built on organic ideas about growth that overtly includes imperfection, specifically, the idea that poetry must be made using "defective means." It is "defective" because it always depends on a single perspective, and because no matter how observant, it must move in one direction only ("Yet there is / no return"). Six times in the first 60 lines of the poem he repeats "rolling up," and, as he did in FMF's elegy, enacting the matter he celebrates. Thus, the first stanza-plus is an exhortation, a direction, and an example:

To make a start,
out of particulars
and make them general, rolling
up the sum, by defective means—
Sniffing the trees,
just another dog
among a lot of dogs. What
else is there? And to do?
The rest have run out—
after the rabbits.
Only the lame stands—on
three legs. Scratch front and back.
Deceive and eat. Dig a musty bone

For the beginning is assuredly
the end—since we know nothing, pure
and simple beyond
our own complexities.

WCW begins (in 1951!) with the process he first expressed as "no ideas / but in things" (in his 1923 poem "A Sort of Song")—that the poem is itself a means of thinking. "Rolling up" is first expressed as a mathematical concept—a "sum"—that poetry is the end result of a process of examining particulars as a dog sniffs trees. Moreover, as he elaborates the dog-sniffing metaphor, the poem stretches out tangentially, conversationally, and embodies the dog's perspective.

A few lines later, he suggests that poetry is like human gestation when he says that "rolling up out of chaos" is "a nine month's wonder" (l. 22), and he dives deeper into this ontogenic (or genetic) metaphor when he compares the process of poetry to a "multiple seed, / packed tight with detail" (l. 31-32). And a third time, at the conclusion of the Preface: he describes "rolling in" as a process that leads from "shells and animalcules / generally and so to man, / in Paterson." (l. 63-65).

His point, a point that he has been making since his chaotic second book *Kora in Hell*, is that poetry must come from a mind that is open, not from a mind that is made up like a bed, and that "defectiveness" and "grossness" are parts of good poetry. His emphasis on "particulars" is not the same as imagism, or haiku. He does not believe in perfect distillation, but in "interpenetration / both ways" and in renewing the self "in addition and subtraction, / walking up and down / and the craft / subverted by thought." His poetics is to trust in the process of examination (the "sniffing"), and to present the articles of that examination where they can reform and regenerate in the mind of the reader. While his parlous, omnivorous style may sometimes take on the incantatory qualities of Walt Whitman—

> the city
> the man, an identity—it can't be
> otherwise—an
> interpenetration, both ways. Rolling
> up! obverse, reverse;
> the drunk the sober; the illustrious
> the gross; one. In ignorance
> a certain knowledge and knowledge,
> undispersed, its own undoing.

—they are different. Whitman's poetics imagines ("bodies forth") a world, and that world is presented whole within the poem. WCW's poetry does not imagine—it examines the world, presents its work almost as a laboratory experiment, where the reader can follow along, and by that process, participate in the open-mindedness WCW trusts.

ARTHUR RUSSELL

WCW's "Young Sycamore"

I want to read this poem once, talk about it a little as it sheds further light on the question how did WCW do his work, what were his methods, what were his aims. And then read it again, see if it has any more traction on our minds.

When I did my last Wms piece, I talked about how Wms wasn't just an imagist. His poems may seem only to be presentations of objects without commentary by the poet, but they are intricately and subtly arguments. So, for example, "The Red Wheelbarrow" may end with wheelbarrow, glazed with rain, white chickens, but it BEGINS with "So much depends upon," which is not only a call to attention but a rhetorical argument for how human life is bound up with the ordinary objects of everyday life.

Same observation here. Whatever else Wms may do in the body of "Young Sycamore," his urgent opening is a part of a story he's telling, a narrative in the form of a portrait. So he begins, "I must tell you," as if he had just run in off the street. But it doesn't stop there; look how the portrait emerges: as his eye travels up the length of the tree from street to top, he uses the words "and then" to make it into a story, and later, "it thins till nothing is left of it." And my point is, isn't it wonderful, how he makes a yarn of a description, because yarns, no matter how short and pithy, are modes of giving human shape to experience, so Wms doesn't have to say "tree is metaphor for human predicament" because the shape of a story told by an urgent messenger does it for him.

And there's more that ties the tree to the human predicament. The story of the tree is a story that mirrors the human story: as it moves upward from a single trunk it rises (and here it is youthful, undulant) (even the reference to splitting "half its height" is like a reference to a kid with his height drawn on the back of a bathroom door), it divides, it wanes, it sends out young branches of its own, like a parent, it grows mossy, maybe even endangered by the "Cocoons" that hang on its branches, and it "thins till nothing is left of it" but these "two / eccentric knotted twigs bending forward hornlike at the top). Who's to say that this doesn't recall, in some intrinsic way, the gnarled features of an old person bending forward).

And focus for a moment on the only simile in the poem: "hornlike" to describe those two uppermost thin twigs. At a minimum, Wms is pulling us towards an animal presence, and as I read it, together with the aging, it's like an old ram or an old bull or an old moose or an old deer.

Next point and it's a doozy. You read this poem and you feel that urgent tale of a boy come in from the rainy spring day with news of the sycamore, and you feel it's a report on nature. Surprise. Well maybe it is, but more immediately, it's actually a description of a photograph taken by Alfred Stieglitz in 1902 called *Spring Showers*— that Wms, who knew Stieglitz, probably saw in one of the galleries that showed his work. This was a proof presented by the literary critic (and art catalog writer) Bram Dijkstra.

So, it's an ekphrastic poem but one in which Wms doesn't see the need to draw attention to the source material, and this gets to the more general point about Wms, that there is no inherent hierarchy of relevance in the objects of the world. A sycamore, a photo of a sycamore and a poem about a sycamore as seen in a photo are all objects worthy of consideration. Stieglitz looked at the tree; Wms looked at the photo of the tree; you and I read a poem about the tree. The poem is a machine made of words for delivering the tree to your mind, to your heart.

JOHN J. TRAUSE

William Carlos Williams and T. S. Eliot United

UNITARIANISM

The Eliots were a Boston family with Puritan roots in Old and New England. Thomas Stearns Eliot's paternal grandfather, William Greenleaf Eliot, had moved to St. Louis, Missouri, to establish a Unitarian Christian church there.

We know that William Carlos Williams's parents were founders of the Unitarian Church in Rutherford, New Jersey, although his father William George Williams was probably originally Anglican, having been born in England, but growing up in the Caribbean, and his mother Raquel Elena Hoheb, born in Puerto Rico of French, Spanish, and Jewish ancestry, was, most likely, originally Roman Catholic.

AVANT-GARDE AND COLLAGE TECHNIQUE

In the penultimate and final chapters (Chapter 22, "Williams and Eliot," pp. 163-174, and Chapter 23, "Conclusion," pp. 175-177) of Wendell Berry's *The Poetry of William Carlos Williams of Rutherford* (Berkeley, Calif.: Counterpoint, 2011), the author seeks to trace out the supposed rivalry between the two poets and reconcile these poets, whose influence on Modernism and all subsequent literature in many languages is immense. The rivalry, seemingly one-sided on Williams's part, starts with Williams's reaction to the publication of *The Waste Land* in 1922. Williams saw Eliot as a literary traitor to America, since the latter was more and more engaged in exploring the European avant-garde instead of cultivating an American idiom based on localism. It is interesting to note that the long poem was published nearly simultaneously in four different venues, two on each side of the Atlantic Ocean. That was long before the days of editors' warning of "no simultaneous submissions" and bidding one to "confirm that this has not appeared in publication in print or online elsewhere." So, drag me to Poetry Court. *The Waste*

Land was the culmination of this exploration and experimentation, and yet both poets are united in their close observation of the local in America, Eliot in his earlier poetry and later in *The Four Quartets*, and Williams throughout his life's work in literature as well as medicine (he lived and practiced medicine in the town of his birth), though Williams studied in Switzerland as a young student and in Germany as a medical specialist in obstetrics and pediatrics. In any case, both poets on close inspection saw the modern world of the early 20th century as a wasteland.

In answer to the prevailing collage technique of Eliot, Ezra Pound, and Gertrude Stein, to name a few American expatriates, not to mention homegrown verbal collagists such as Marianne Moore, even Williams employed this appropriative method of composition, smacking of the European avant-garde, in his masterpiece, *Paterson*. The impresario Daniel P. Quinn, in his annual Great George Festival in Paterson, New Jersey (1996; 1998-2001), produced a sequential staged reading of each book of *Paterson*, one per year, rightly employing a panel of various actors assigned the various voices in the polyphonic text of each book.

COMMON THEMES

Wendell Berry also demonstrates how Williams and Eliot also share the same themes in their poetry, whether it is concepts of old versus new, utopia versus the wasteland, or even the Visit of the Magi as a subject.

I, too, have found that both Williams and Eliot looked at and were moved by the same painting, Jean-Honoré Fragonard's *L'Escarpolette* (*The Swing*, ca. 1767), so much so that each made reference to it in one of their poems—"Mr. Apollinax" [1917] by T. S. Eliot and "Portrait Of A Lady" [1920] by William Carlos Williams—each getting the citation wrong with a little poetic license. I make reference to and provide a corrective to both of them in my poem about getting a haircut, "Snip Snip Snip," written in 1985 and published in *The Rutherford Red Wheelbarrow* no. 4 (2011), as well as in my book, *Exercises in High Treason* (New York: great weather for

MEDIA, 2016). This is my little way of uniting these giants of Modernism.

"Mr. Apollinax" [1917] by T. S. Eliot (1888 – 1965)

Ω της καινοτητος 'Ηρακλεις, της παραδοξολογιας ευμηχανος ανθρωπος.
                                                              —Lucian

WHEN Mr. Apollinax visited the United States
His laughter tinkled among the teacups.
I thought of Fragilion, that shy figure among the birch-trees,
And of Priapus in the shrubbery
Gaping at the lady in the swing.
In the palace of Mrs. Phlaccus, at Professor Channing-Cheetah's
He laughed like an irresponsible fœtus.
His laughter was submarine and profound
Like the old man of the sea's
Hidden under coral islands
Where worried bodies of drowned men drift down in the green silence,
Dropping from fingers of surf.
I looked for the head of Mr. Apollinax rolling under a chair
Or grinning over a screen
With seaweed in its hair.
I heard the beat of centaur's hoofs over the hard turf
As his dry and passionate talk devoured the afternoon.
"He is a charming man"—"But after all what did he mean?"—
"His pointed ears . . . He must be unbalanced,"—
"There was something he said that I might have challenged."
Of dowager Mrs. Phlaccus, and Professor and Mrs. Cheetah
I remember a slice of lemon, and a bitten macaroon.

Eliot, Thomas Stearns. *Prufrock and Other Observations*. From *Poems*. New York: A. A. Knopf, 1920; Bartleby.com, 2011.

"Portrait of a Lady" [1920] by William Carlos Williams (1883-1963)

Your thighs are appletrees
whose blossoms touch the sky.
Which sky? The sky
where Watteau hung a lady's
slipper. Your knees
are a southern breeze—or
a gust of snow. Agh! what
sort of man was Fragonard?
—As if that answered
anything.—Ah, yes. Below
the knees, since the tune
drops that way, it is
one of those white summer days,
the tall grass of your ankles
flickers upon the shore—
Which shore?—
the sand clings to my lips—
Which shore?
Agh, petals maybe. How
should I know?
Which shore? Which shore?
Which shore?
I said petals from an appletree.

Williams, William Carlos. *Collected Poems of William Carlos Williams.*
New York: New Directions, 1986-1988.

MARK FOGARTY

Coming into His Own

Ambassadors of the Silenced, by Alfred Encarnacion. Kelsay Books.

I read a lot of poetry. I'm the managing editor of the fine anthology *The Rutherford Red Wheelbarrow* (ten volumes out to date) and have reviewed 20 books for this anthology and attheinkwell.com. Alfred Encarnacion's *Ambassadors of the Silenced* is the best book of poetry I've read in a long time.

Ambassadors of the Silenced is a big book, in terms of theme, emotional arc and even page count. Its theme is the awful rowing a "mestizo" like Encarnacion (he had a Filipino-American father and European mother) has to do to come into his own as a person and a poet in America. By evidence of this book, he certainly has come into his own as a poet.

His is actually a multi-generational story that begins with Encarnacion wishing he had a photo of his Filipino grandfather to help him invent a face that would show something more than his own "unheroic life" in America. Then it proceeds to his father, an immigrant "Pinoy" who has come to America and gets dubbed with the decidedly unheroic nickname of "Freddie Donuts." (Filipina-Americans are called "Pinays.") In the garish San Francisco Filipino "Flip Town," he moves among street girls with "skin as white as heroin."

Encarnacion's father marries a white woman but soon abandons the family. Encarnacion grows up with an abusive stepfather, or "my mother's husband" as he refers to him. As a child he soon realizes his situation: "a postwar baby / with slanted eyes, chubby cheeks, / and waves of squid-black hair." He describes himself as a "dark and sullen boy" "praying for some private transformation."

So far, Encarnacion has been unlucky with fathers. But then his luck changes with the discovery of a Pinoy writer he can identify with. Carlos Bulosan is about his father's age and the author of a wonderfully titled book called *America Is in the Heart*. The section of the book called "Ambassadors of the Silenced" is a fine series of poems imagining Bulosan's hardscrabble existence and "lonely art" where he learns "that in many ways it was a crime to be a Filipino."

Encarnacion, who has written knowledgeably about music in his first book, *The Outskirts of Karma*, links Bulosan's wanderings to those of the grand, itinerant American bluesman Robert Johnson and imagines a postcard from jail as starting, "I wake up today at six o'clock, / a clot of sunrise stuck / to the windows like blood." Blood, the hallmark of tuberculosis, will soon claim Bulosan in his mid forties, but credit Encarnacion for finding a pure American spirit and a fine literary muse who should be much better known than he is. *America Is in the Heart* would be a fine alternate title for *Ambassadors of the Silenced*.

Encarnacion credits Bulosan with reconciling him with his father, and he recalls an old Filipino story about a farmer whose family has deserted him and who is visited by a flock of *tikgi* birds who eventually transform themselves into his lost family. The poet's engagement with Bulosan seems to reconcile him somewhat with his family and his emotional journey to connect as an American.

But from this hopeful midterm, life ensues. "Winter Light" is a series of poems about the death of his mother. He uses the image of a diving bell rising from the water (from a long-ago trip to Atlantic City, where he hoped to see a shark) to evoke the dying spirits rising to their deaths. This time, he can see the shark fin. And he gets to feel "how the dead / insinuate themselves / in the minds of the / living with such / tender bravado."

Things aren't much better in the final section of the book, "After the Summer." There are poems with titles like "No Map Can Hold the Wind" (about the Holocaust) and a landscape that features a moon "red / as a burning / tire." Incongruous images like an obit of someone that lists one of his survivors as "Dildo" the dog (hilarious!) help inform this judgement: "Sadness pervades this life, but who / needs another sob story?"

Being a poet often means being fucked up. It is how you deal with it that puts you on the spectrum between Dildo the Dog and Freddie Donuts and the heroic Bulosan. Encarnacion chooses

Bulosan's road in an extraordinary final poem invoking Bo Diddley. The old rocker, inventor of his own much-imitated heartbeat, evokes the mestizo life in the fictional town of "Hong Kong, Mississippi." Robert Johnson lopes in again, hellhound on his trail, but the itinerant poet isn't looking to make a diabolical deal at Johnson's famous crossroad. He is interested in what's down one of those roads, a "town lost / in the fields of cotton" where "Buddha transcends the blues."

MARK FOGARTY

A Sense of Place

Meta-Land: Poets of the Palisades II. The Poet's Press.

It would make sense that a poetry collection from writers based on or near the basaltic Palisades formation would be concerned with place (and perhaps with hardness, too). But it's not just Northern New Jersey these poetic geologists are probing.

There's a good bit of metaphysical inquiry going on as well, apt for a book with "meta" in its title (with a second reference being a pun on the local New Jersey Meadowlands).

So the late Brant Lyon's poem "Skia Has a Heart-to-Heart with Plato Outside the Cave" carries on an erudite conversation with Plato, complete with a footnote for those who slept through philosophy class. And the maker of the universe gets some attention, too, as in David Messineo's "Jesus at 16," in which the adolescent Jesus gives his Father a little backtalk. And Denise Rue muses that the means of talking with God, prayer, is like a gadget, a pulley or a hook. It is kind of comforting that the end of her "How it Might Work" names "God the clockmaker once more / you his immaculate machine."

Meta-Land is a handsomely made book, the second to come out of a nexus of poets who meet at the Classic Quiche in Teaneck, NJ. There are lots of poets in *Meta-Land* that you will see in the anthology you are holding: John Barrale, who locates Jesus' grandmother St. Anne in Canada; Anton Yakovlev, Don Zirilli, John J. Trause, Joel Allegretti, Catharine Cavallone, Josh Humphrey, Davidson Garrett,

Paul Nash, Denise La Neve. I like John Barrale's reporting of a traditional and quite utilitarian prayer some of the Canadians offer to St. Anne de Beaupre: "I beg you, holy mother Anne, send me a good and loving man."

Editors Nash, La Neve, Messineo, Susanna Rich and Trause have put together a big book, 121 poems by 58 poets (and some artwork) grouped into sections with one-word titles like "Surviving" or "Living." As with all anthologies, there are some poems that don't do much for me, but then I'm struck by ones that do.

So here is master poet Maria Mazzioti Gillan writing in "The Cup" about her life as a fragile china cup "so fine that my fingers show through / as pale blue shadows." Poems aren't usually spellbinding, but take Humphrey's "The Twenty Four Hours." A mother is talking to a son who has been struck by a thrown discus and must not be allowed to fall asleep for 24 hours, lest he slip into a coma.

The parent starts her monologue with comforting, quotidian details like "This is the planet Earth" and "I am your mother." But soon it is the mother who could use a little comforting, wandering off into stressed-out tangents like "Your brother's wife is ugly" or what it was like when she made love (inappropriate, but mom's pretty freaked out by now).

Poetry often takes itself too seriously, but not Christi Shannon Kline's "Nonsense," a delightful rhyme whose title may tip off its intentions. A meditation on mayonnaise by Elissa Gordon also had a light touch, though a harder payoff. I was moved by Messineo's "To Be Or Not To Be," an elegy for Tyler Clementi, a New Jersey boy bullied into suicide.

If I have a favorite it is "Why the World Doesn't End" by Tina Kelley. It starts "We'll die in ignorance" and proceeds to tick off a few of the many unknowables. The consolation? "Someone of mine will be here to know." Here's a lovely thought: "The urges to learn and reproduce / sit on the same gene." The someone of mine is quite close, at the breast in fact, "looking more fetal than fierce," though "The universe is telling her secrets."

That's better than finding out the last decimal of *pi,* don't you think?

LOREN KLEINMAN

Interview with Jim Klein

Indie Reader.com
The Huffington Post Book Blog
2014

ABOUT THE WRITER

Like most writers my age I wanted to be Hemingway. Also like many, I thought I should be an English professor to have time to write. Then it seemed like a good idea to have a Ph.D. so I wouldn't get bossed around by people who just had M.A.s. At the University of Illinois, I took a lot of boring courses and requirements and learned more and more about less and less (John Barth) until I met a friend who really fired me up and I had a manic episode and did a lot of crazy things, and felt guilty, and decided to do what I wanted, and started on poetry when I was about 30, because I didn't know anything about it, and I determined to lose my ignorance strategically, which I am still doing. If I hadn't been kind of a nice, underachieving kid of German parents, I would have gone straight to the Village because I think I am pretty much self-taught as a poet.

WHY DID I CHOOSE POETRY

By the time I finished the dissertation on John Barth, I knew I didn't want to write fiction. Life is what happens while you're planning other things, and I had written exactly one short story. Burroughs, in *Naked Lunch,* talks about how slow having characters is, and getting them to the airport, etc. I loved the idea of poetry as the best words in the best order. I immediately embraced the idea that every poem had something to teach me if I could push it as far as it would go. The impossibility was an attraction. I had had the experience of trying to explain my manic ideas to people who couldn't understand them. I distrusted the spoken word. Language should be used by lovers for amusement only. My best friends were Harry Walsh and Mike O'Brien, and we had a new poem in our back pocket every day at lunch at Stan's. Any day we wrote a new poem was a good day.

WHERE DO I GET MY INSPIRATION

Amateurs believe in inspiration. All any artist has to do is to show up for work, preferably on a regular schedule. Don't get me started on "prompts." Nothing should be written that doesn't need to be done. My father told me you have two capacities: creative and critical. The secret is to separate them. Pull it out of your ass sideways, and then see what you've got. Separate the synthetic capacity from the critical; protect the right brain from the left, and then reverse polarities. I had a background in newspapers, so I was used to writing as fast as I could type. The brain is an elephant with the little guy on top the consciousness. To find out what the elephant is up to start typing and keep going. When you're stuck write "I'm stuck." Write why you can't write and how you feel about it. Do a row of nines. Write in rhythm with the music or to the TV. I found George Bush good to write to. At some point, you'll write a good sentence. A true sentence. You will feel the traction. Keep going: that's the pome coming through. Throw the stuff above it away. That's when and where you were trying to write a poem. Now you are writing what you have to write. It'll have veins of rhyme and rhythm all through. This will be what Williams told Ginsberg was "live language." Pound's theory was that the value of rhyme was that it forced you to bounce around in your unconscious where you didn't expect to go. I have a wireless keyboard now, so I can write lying down and not even see the result.

WHAT BOOK AM I CURRENTLY READING

Art Since 1900, Foster, Krauss, Bois, Buchloh. I mostly read about art now because I am trying to be a painter. Also, I find reading about poetry pretty boring. Most poetry, too, if the truth be known. I'm bipolar. I'm wired hotter than most people. I find the fast manic action of painting more in tune with my makeup. I'm trying to get bigger right now. I'm painting to *Yeesus*. Pollock said it all when he talked about being "in the painting." You have to be in the poem. But in poetry, you can spend years making it better. In painting I know when I can't make it better. I go for what Fischl calls "the frozen moment" when anything I add will only make it worse.

Jamison, *Touched with Fire*, says you create on manics and revise when you are depressed. I know I'm probably better at poetry so far than painting, so I revise poems all week and paint on Saturdays. Right now, I'm afraid to start new poems because they will distract me. The point is not to have a lot of poems, which I have, but to have great poems. My new theory of writing is that the real audience for a poem is not a reading or a publication but the poem itself: it is looking back at you like a face in the mirror, it knows what it could be, and it's saying, "Is that all you got? Is that all you got?"

The fascinating thing I just read in Foster et al, if anybody still cares, is that Pollock's radicalism was immediately tamed by the critics after de Kooning's first show. *"In many ways, the subservience of de Kooning's white-on-black canvases to Pollock's most recent development was a kiss of death: gone was the looseness and risk-taking of the drip technique, now replaced by a tight grip on the brush and nervous twists of the wrist."* I never went to poetry school. I just started doing it and doing it and after awhile the theory caught up with the practice. I've been painting about eight years now and finally the theory is catching up with my practice. I'm going to try to take on the abstract expressionist counter-revolutionaries.

The pernt is that the writer should write and the theory will catch up sometime. But it hardly ever works that way. Most people start with a theory or get strangled in the cradle by well-meaning people trying to help with a theory.

IS THERE ANYTHING ELSE I'D LIKE TO ADD

"There are leaders and followers,
I'd rather be a dick than a swallower." —Kanye West

Contributors

Joel Allegretti

Joel Allegretti is the author of, most recently, *Platypus: Poems—Prose—Performance Texts* (NYQ Books, 2017) and a novella, *Our Dolphin* (Thrice Publishing, 2016). He is the editor of *Rabbit Ears: TV Poems* (NYQ Books, 2015).

Amy Barone

Amy Barone's new poetry collection, *We Became Summer*, from New York Quarterly Books, will be released in 2018. She wrote chapbooks *Kamikaze Dance* (Finishing Line Press) and *Views from the Driveway* (Foothills Publishing.) Her poetry has appeared in *Gradiva*, *Paterson Literary Review*, and *Sensitive Skin*. She belongs to PEN America Center and the brevitas online poetry community. From Bryn Mawr, PA, Amy lives in New York City.

John Barrale

John Barrale's poetry has been published in numerous print and online publications and has won several awards. Most recently, his poems have appeared in *Unrorean, East Meets West—American Writers Review, Icon, Narrative Northeast, Pidgeonholes, and Sensations Magazine*. In June 2012, *Shakespeare's Moths*, a collection of John's early poems, was published by *White Chickens Press*. John is also the curator of *The Poetry Exchange*, a free electronic community bulletin board that announces poetry and literary events in the NY/NJ area. Along with four other "Gang of Five" members, John hosts a monthly poetry reading series at The William Carlos Williams Center in Rutherford, NJ. John is also one of the managing editors of *The Rutherford Red Wheelbarrow*.

R. Bremner

R. Bremner has guested six-times on the Poetry Super Highway radio show, where he has served as Poet of the Week, and has been featured at *Poets Online* twenty times. Bremner has twice received honorable mention in the Allen Ginsberg Poetry Awards. Always the bridesmaid, never the bride, Ron vows to win the grand prize next year. You can find his famous and fabulous eBooks, *You are once again the stranger* and *Kerouac Dreams, Kerouac Visions*, at Amazon, Barnes and Noble, Lulu, Smashwords, Kobo, or the iBookstore.

Marian Calabro

Marian Calabro has been a popular writing workshop leader at the Adult School of Montclair for more than ten years. The author of 20 nonfiction history books, including the award-winning *Perilous Journey of the Donner Party*, Marian Calabro is also a business owner, a published poet and aspiring playwright. www.mariancalabro.com.

Cathy Cavallone

Cathy Cavallone studied at Montclair State University and currently teaches English. She has been featured at local venues such as the Classic Quiche in Teaneck and at the Williams Center for the Arts in Rutherford. Her work has been published in *The Rutherford Red Wheelbarrow, The New Verse News, Turk's Head Review, Rose Red Review, Nerve Lantern*, and others. She is a Pushcart Prize nominee and lives with her husband and son in North Jersey.

John Dull

John Dull is a poet/singer/songwriter whose family has been involved in the folk music community for 30+ years. Dull has performed with Pete Seeger; Richie Havens; Peter, Paul and Mary; Emmylou Harris; Tom Paxton and others. www.dullmusic.com.

D. M. Dutcher

D. M. Dutcher writes in New Jersey where he has directed and hosted three poetry reading series, making them distinctive by writing essay introductions for the featured poets discussing various aspects of their writing. He has supported his muse as a fine woodworker and carpenter and working in a professional theater creating stage sets.

Milton P. Ehrlich

Milton P. Ehrlich, Ph.D., is an 85-year-old psychologist and a veteran of the Korean War who has published numerous poems in periodicals such as *Descant, Ottawa Arts Review, Wisconsin Review, Allegro Poetry Magazine, Toronto Quarterly Review, Christian Science Monitor, Huffington Post*, and *The New York Times*.

Alfred Encarnacion

Alfred Encarnacion's poems, short stories, essays, and reviews have appeared in national journals— such as *Crab Orchard Review, Florida Review, Indiana Review, North American Review, The Paterson Literary Review*, and the online Virtual Artists Collective—and his work has been anthologized in *Blues Poems, Identity Lessons, The Open Boat: Poems from Asian America*, and *Unsettling America. The Outskirts of Karma*, his debut collection of poetry, was published in the spring of 2012. *Ambassadors of the Silenced* is his second.

Gil Fagiani

Gil Fagiani's latest book is *Logos* (Guernica Editions, 2015). Gil co-hosts the Italian American Writers' Association's monthly readings in Manhattan. In 2014, he was the subject of a *New York Times* article by David Gonzalez, "A Poet Mines Memories of Drug Addiction."

John L. Fogarty

John L. Fogarty has done several English-to-Irish translations. He is Director of Capital Planning at Stony Brook University.

Mark Fogarty

Mark Fogarty is a poet, musician, and journalist from Rutherford, NJ. One of the managing editors of *The Rutherford Red Wheelbarrow*, he emcees the monthly reading at GainVille Café in Rutherford. He has had poetry in more than 20 publications. Mark is the author of six books of poetry from White Chickens Press: *Myshkin's Blues*, *Peninsula*, *Phantom Engineer*, *Sun Nets*, *Continuum: The Jaco Poems*, and *The Tall Women's Dance: Poems on Women's Basketball*.

Davidson Garrett

Davidson Garrett is a poet, actor, and New York City yellow taxi driver. His latest chapbook is titled *What Happened To The Man Who Taught Me Beowulf and Other Poems* (Advent Purple Press).

Gordon A. Gilbert, Jr.

A longtime NYC West Villager, Gordon Gilbert performs his poetry, songs, and monologues in the metropolitan area. He also has written short stories and aplay, *Monologues from the Old Folks Home*, produced 8 times at various NYC venues. Gordon hosts poetry readings in NYC and an annual September reading, *Remembrances of 9/11*.

Gia Grillo

Gia Grillo is a poet living and working in Lyndhurst, N.J., where she has helped run workshops for local students with a focus on making poetry a cathartic and accessible art form. She has most recently been published in *The Battering Ram*, *The Veg*, and *Virga*.

Pamela Hughes

Pamela Hughes has a BA from Fairleigh Dickinson University and MFA in Creative Writing (poetry) from Brooklyn College, where she studied with Allen Ginsberg. Her poetry has been in numerous journals and magazines. Pamela is the editor of *Narratives Northeast*, an online poetry and literary journal. Her book *Meadowland Take My Hand* was published by Three Mile Harbor Press in 2017.

Josh Humphrey

Josh Humphrey has lived in and around Kearny, NJ, for all of his life, and he continues to spend his days there as the local Library Director. This year, he published *Afterlife*, his first chapbook of poems, which includes the beautiful photography of his father, Bill Humphrey.

Gail King

Gail King is now working on two new books of poetry. One she is calling *The Memory Wall*. The other will be called *Poet in Motion*.

Melanie Klein

Melanie Klein is the author of a chapbook, *There Was a Gathering Darkness* (2010, Errant Pigeon Press) and is active in the Visual Poets, a 5-person art-making group based in Poughkeepsie, NY. She earned an M.F.A. at the City College of New York, where she was awarded the Jerome Lowell DeJur Prize in Poetry. Her poems have appeared in *The Rutherford Red Wheelbarrow, Right Hand Pointing, Otoliths*, and elsewhere.

Jim Klein

Jim Klein is editor-in-chief of *The Red Wheelbarrow* and the moderator of The Red Wheelbarrow Workshop—Rutherford, NJ's iconic poetry workshop that has met weekly since 2005. Jim's poetry has been published in *Beloit Poetry Journal*, *Berkeley Poetry Review*, *College English*, *The Wormwood Review*, and numerous other publications. In 2007, Jim's manuscript *I Didn't Know If I Was Afoot or on Horseback* was a finalist in the Anthony Hecht Award Competition and in the Sawtooth Poetry Prize. Jim is the author of *Blue Chevies* (White Chickens Press, 2008), *To Eat Is Human, Digest Divine* (White Chickens Press, 2010), and a chapbook, *Trinis Talk Like Birds* (Errant Pigeon Press, 2011).

Janet Kolstein

Janet Kolstein's poetry has been published in *Instigatorzine*, *Lips*, *The Poetry of Place: North Jersey in Poetry*, *The Rutherford Red Wheelbarrow*, and *The Newstead Abbey Byron Society Review*. Janet is a member of *The Byron Society of America* and has traveled to St. Andrews, Scotland, and Boston, MA, for conferences on the poet. Janet is a member of the International Byron Society. She is also an artist who exhibits her work in the Tri-State area, and she is a member of the hob'art cooperative gallery in Hoboken, NJ.

Melene Kubat

Melene Kubat is a resident of Oakland, NJ, who has been enjoying a brief sabbatical (oops, lay-off!) after many years with Pearson Education. She has long loved the arts, particularly poetry, art, literature, music, and film. Her poems have appeared in *The Red Wheelbarrow* #9, and she has exhibited her artwork at *Art in the Park* at Van Saun Park in Paramus, NJ, for the past few years.

Denise La Neve

Denise La Neve writes both poetry and fiction. She was a contributor and editor for the 2016 meta-anthology *META-LAND* (The Poet's Press). Her most recent work has been published in *Platform Review* (Spring 2017), *Quill and Parchment*, and *The Rutherford Red Wheelbarrow* #9, and will soon appear in *Exit 13*. Denise co-hosts the longstanding North Jersey Literary Series (Teaneck, NJ) with her husband, Paul Nash, and she is currently writing a chapbook inspired by her childhood experiences in Citers, France.

Susanna Lee

Susanna Lee published *Sunrise Mountain*, her first book of haiku and other poetry, in 2015. She shares poetry anywhere friends or random strangers meet, in libraries, bars, and cafés, and often at Writers' Roundtable, Thursdays Are for Poetry, Tea and Conversation, Sussex Bards, Sensations Magazine, Red Wheelbarrow Poets, Pagoda Writers, North Jersey Literary Series, Great Weather For Media, GainVille Café, Carriage House, brevitas, and on her sun porch.

Stuart Leonard

Stuart Leonard has been active in the New Jersey poetry scene for several decades. His poem *Taking Brooklyn Bridge* was published by the Occupied Media Pamphlet Series in 2011. He has also been published in *Exit 13* (2015) and *The Rutherford Red Wheelbarrow #9* (2016). Most recently, he received an honorable mention in the Allen Ginsberg Poetry Awards.

Frances Lombardi-Grahl

Frances Lombardi-Grahl became involved in poetry when she joined the Bergen Poets in the late '70s. Her poetry has been published in *Paterson Literary Review*, *Lips*, and *Italian Americana*. Frances attends workshops at the Red Wheelbarrow Poets and is appreciative of their support and friendship. Frances teaches ESL at various locations.

Addie Mahmassani

Addie Mahmassani is a student in the Rutgers Newark American Studies Ph.D. program. She studies cultural history of the 20th century, with an emphasis on live popular performance. She is also a singer, with an EP entitled *Believe the Birds* out now. These are the first poems she has published.

Michael Mandzik

Michael Mandzik began writing poetry during the 1970s, with poems published in the Fordham University *Monthly*, *Corduroy*, and the Montclair State College *Quarterly* (the last both in print and on vinyl). Mike's workshop studies have included Diane Wakoski, Edwin Romond, Maureen Seaton, BJ Ward, and most recently the Red Wheelbarrow Poets. Mike is NJ born and raised; he resides with his family in western Essex County.

Elinor Mattern

Elinor Mattern's poems and non-fiction have appeared in journals and newspapers including *Washington Square*, *Footwork*, *Paterson Literary Review*, and *The Philadelphia Inquirer*. She is also a visual artist, exhibits her work, and presents workshops on many aspects of culture, creativity, and communication.

Leilani McInerney

Leilani writes of herself the following: "Whether we write it, think it, pronounce it or sing it, poetry pervades our lives. It is as essential as the air we breathe and the sun that warms us. In my working life, a professional actress and singer in New York, followed by 12 years of teaching, my poems have been published in *The Rutherford Red Wheelbarrow*, *The South Bergenite*, and *The Record*. After featuring at *Thursdays Are for Poetry* in Teaneck, my writings debuted in New York at The Cornelia Street Cafe *Monologues and Madness* program and with the Irish American Writers & Artists Salon at The Cell Theatre, also in New York. A NJ resident for over 40 years, an avid gardener and dog owner, 'I write for balance and for the sheer fun of it.'"

Wayne L. Miller

Wayne L. Miller is a writer and poet from Northern New Jersey. His work has been published in *Arc Poetry Magazine, Paterson Literary Review, LIPS, Turtle Island Quarterly, theNewerYork, Narrative Northeast, The Long-Islander* (Walt's Corner), *Instigatorzine, Edison Literary Review, Exit 13, Cattails, Midnight Circus*, and several anthologies.

Zorida Mohammed

Zorida Mohammed was born in Trinidad and emigrated to America at age 18. She has a M.S.W. from Fordham University School of Social Work and has worked as a Social Worker in NJ for the past 26 years. Zorida's poems have been published in *The Caribbean Writer, Folio, Poem, Atlanta Review, The Spoon River Poetry Review, Fulcrum # 6* and *7, Phoebe, Oyez Review, Compass Rose, The Dirty Goat # 20, Bayou Magazine, The Distillery*, and *Quercus Review*. Zorida was a recipient of the New Jersey State Council on the Arts grant for poetry in 1991-92; is a member of the Red Wheelbarrow Poets; has been a featured reader at FDU, Englewood, and the Rutherford libraries; and has read her poetry in many venues in NY and NJ.

Bill Moreland

Bill Moreland marks his first publication of poetry anywhere with 4 entries in the RWB #10. He is a husband for 35 years to Sandi; father to three beautiful children, Valerie, Juline, and Gary; grandfather to one, Charlotte Rose; and a life-long New Jersey resident and professional salesperson for Salem Press, publishers of reference materials.

Bob Murken

Now retired and living in Philadelphia, Bob taught poetry for 35 years but got around to writing it only six years ago. Bob also taught high school English and German in Louisville, Baltimore, and Orangeburg.

Paul Nash

Paul Nash is a naturalist, writer, and editor whose published works include scientific and historical articles, poetry, essays, and narrative fiction. He studies ancient insects in amber at the American Museum of Natural History, and his travels have taken him all over the globe. Paul co-hosts the North Jersey Literary Series (Teaneck, NJ) with his wife, Denise La Neve, and contributed to / edited the 2016 anthology *META-LAND*. His poetry has most recently appeared in the journal *Quill and Parchment* (2016) and will soon be published in *The Bug Book* (Poets Wear Prada, 2017), for which he also wrote the foreword.

James B. Nicola

James B. Nicola's poems have appeared in the *Antioch, Southwest,* and *Atlanta Reviews, Rattle, Tar River,* and *Poetry East.* His nonfiction book *Playing the Audience* won a *Choice* award. His first full-length poetry collection is *Manhattan Plaza* (2014); his second, *Stage to Page: Poems from the Theater* (June 2016). A Yale graduate, James has been giving both theater and poetry workshops at libraries, literary festivals, schools, and community centers all over the country— particularly in New Jersey.

Michael O'Brien

Michael O'Brien is a retired professor of English. He is the author of a poetry collection, *Absence Implies Presence.* His poems and reviews have appeared in *The Literary Review, Lunch, Muse-Pie Press, Poet, Lips, Context South,* and numerous other journals. He has read his poetry throughout NJ and was featured at the William Carlos Williams Center and at the Geraldine R. Dodge Poetry Festival. He lives in Bloomingdale, NJ, with his wife Moira Shaw O'Brien.

Jennifer Poteet

Jennifer Poteet is a longtime Montclair, NJ, resident and works in Manhattan as a fundraiser for public television. Her poems have appeared in numerous online and print journals, most recently *Clementine Unbound*, *The Cortland Review*, and *Pedestal Magazine*. Her first chapbook, *Sleepwalking Home,* will be published in the fall of 2017 by Dancing Girl Press.

Daniel P. Quinn

Award-winning author and playwright Daniel P. Quinn's books include *Exits and Entrances: Producing Off-Broadway, Opera and Beyond*, and *Organized Labor: Poems of Life, Death and Love*. Daniel's plays appear in *Short Plays to Long Remember* (TNT Books). He is the director of ArtsPRunlimited Inc. Daniel has received grants and awards from the Irish Institute, The NY Times Company Foundation, Axe-Houghton Foundation, The New York State Council of the Arts, The Short Play Festival, and The Actor's Fund. Daniel also received a scholarship for the Non-profit Executive and Emerging Leader Certificate Program at Rutgers University in Newark, NJ.

Della Rowland

Della Rowland has always lived by a river and written by a window, her best poetic inspirations. As a youth she left the heartland for NYC where, in addition to various and often very odd jobs, she was an editor at *Ms. Magazine*, Scholastic, Time Inc, and several children's publishing companies. She's published some 40 children's books and taught elementary writing as Artist-in-Residence for 15 years. In 2005, she founded the William Carlos Williams Poetry Symposium, which has produced major events in Rutherford, NJ, to commemorate the life and work of the poet/doctor in his hometown.

Arthur Russell

Arthur Russell lives in Nutley, NJ. He has worked as a salesman at Gimbel's Department Store in Herald Square, tender operator at Miramar YC, NYC taxicab driver, cook, bricklayer's assistant, car wash manager, and, since 1988, attorney. His poem "The Whales Off Manhattan Beach Breaching In Winter" was Brooklyn Poets' Poem of the Year for 2015 and received Honorable Mention in the Allen Ginsberg Poetry Awards for 2016. His poems have appeared in *Paterson Literary Review*, *The Yellow Chair Review*, and *The Brooklyn Poets Anthology* and have been accepted for publication by *Prelude*.

Dan Saxon

Dan Saxon has been writing and publishing since the early 1960s, when he contributed to and published *Poets at Le Metro*. Dan's poems have appeared in several magazines and anthologies including *The East Side Scene: American Poetry, 1960-1965* (Anchor Doubleday, 1972), and *In a Time of Revolution: Poems from our Third World* (Random House, 1969). Dan's most recent poetry collection is *Linked Robins* (Xlibris, 2008).

Claudia Serea

Claudia Serea is a Romanian-born poet who immigrated to the U.S. in 1995. Her poems and translations have appeared in *Field*, *New Letters*, *5 a.m.*, *Meridian*, *Word Riot*, *Apple Valley Review*, among others. Serea is the author of *Angels & Beasts* (Phoenicia Publishing, Canada, 2012), *A Dirt Road Hangs From the Sky* (8th House Publishing, Canada, 2013), *To Part Is to Die a Little* (Cervena Barva Press, 2015), and *Nothing Important Happened Today* (Broadstone Books, 2016). Serea co-hosts The Williams Readings poetry series in Rutherford, NJ. She is a founding editor of *National Translation Month*. More at cserea.tumblr.com.

Zev Shanken

Zev Shanken lives in Teaneck, NJ, and currently teaches English at Kean College and the College of Staten Island. He is a co-curator of the Thursdays Are for Poetry reading series and serves on the steering committee of *brevitas*, a writers' group dedicated to the short poem. Zev's chapbook *Al Het* is available from Blue Begonia Press, and his full-length poetry collection *Memory Ticks* is available from Full Court Press.

Ria Torricelli

Ria Torricelli is thrilled to have her poetry published for the first time in *The Rutherford Red Wheelbarrow* #10. An actor and improvisational comedian with ComedySportz Worldwide, Ria recently moved back to New Jersey and is currently trying to decide what she wants to be when she grows up. Other writing credits include "The Grumpy Hiker," a newspaper column for the sarcastic traveler. Special thanks to Tom, whose spirited sense of adventure led her to meet this talented group of poets.

John J. Trause

John J. Trause, the Director of Oradell Public Library, is the author of *Why Sing?* (Sensitive Skin Press, 2017), a book of traditional and experimental poems; *Picture This: For Your Eyes and Ears* (Dos Madres Press, 2016*)*, a book of poems on art, film, and photography; *Exercises in High Treason* (great weather for MEDIA, 2016), a book of fictive translations, found poems, and manipulated texts; *Eye Candy for Andy* (*13 Most Beautiful... Poems for Andy Warhol's Screen Tests*, Finishing Line Press, 2013); *Inside Out, Upside Down, and Round and Round* (Nirala Publications, 2012); *Seriously Serial* (Poets Wear Prada, 2007; rev. ed. 2014); and *Latter-Day Litany* (Éditions élastiques, 1996), the latter staged Off Broadway. His translations, poetry, and visual work appear internationally in many journals and anthologies, including the artists' periodical

Crossings, the Dada journal *Maintenant*, the journal *Offerta Speciale*, the Great Weather for Media anthologies *It's Animal but Merciful* (2012) and *I Let Go of the Stars in My Hand* (2014), and *Rabbit Ears*: *TV Poems* (NYQ Books, 2015). Marymark Press has published his visual poetry and art as broadsides and sheets. He is a founder of the William Carlos Williams Poetry Cooperative in Rutherford, NJ, and the former host and curator of its monthly reading series. He is fond of cunning acrostics and color-coded chiasmus.

Alice Twombly

Alice Twombly, who shows that there is nothing like retirement to keep you working at things you love, is the Co-Curator of *Thursdays Are for Poetry* at Classic Quiche. An early founder of *Salute to Women in the Arts,* she was involved in collaborations between poetry and dance. Her poems have been published in the *NJ Poetry Monthly,* where she was a State winner, *First Literary Review-East,* and *The Rutherford Red Wheelbarrow* #9. She has also won prizes for her photography and has appeared in one-woman and group shows in the NJ-NY Metro area. Since 2011, she has given a variety of lecturers on literary topics at the Teaneck (NJ) Library's Friday Morning Group, and she has taught at the Learning Collaborative of the New City Jewish Center, an adult college, since 2010. She became a member of *brevitas* in 2017.

Ken Vennette

Ken Vennette spent most of his life in rural upstate New York working in the building trades as a carpenter / cabinetmaker. He is currently an assistant Professor of English and Humanities, as well Humanities Division Chair, at Fulton-Montgomery Community College in Johnstown, NY. Ken has a Master's Degree in English, specializing in Creative Non-Fiction, from the College of Saint Rose in Albany, NY. He is the author of a chapbook, *Illegitimi non Carborundum* (Errant Pigeon Press, 2017).

Barbara R. Williams-Hubbard

Barbara R. Williams-Hubbard is a poet, singer, and former teacher of Church History and English as a Second Language, whose past work includes real estate, advertising, and law. Barbara holds a B.A. in Bible, Theology, English, and Education from Gordon College, Wenham, MA, and a Masters in Communication Arts from William Paterson University, Wayne, NJ. She is a North Jersey Literary Series Featured Poet and a three-time award-winner at the annual Saint Catherine of Bologna's Patron of the Arts Exhibition (Ringwood, NJ). Barbara's poems have appeared in *Sensations Magazine*, *The Great Falls*, *The Rutherford Red Wheelbarrow*, and others.

Anton Yakovlev

Anton Yakovlev's latest poetry collection is *Ordinary Impalers* (Aldrich Press, 2017). His poems have appeared in *The New Yorker*, *The Hopkins Review*, *Prelude*, *Measure*, and elsewhere. *The Last Poet of the Village*, a book of translations of poetry by Sergei Esenin, was published by Sensitive Skin Books in 2017.

Nicole Zach

Nicole Zach is from Lyndhurst, NJ. Writing poetry since 1996, she has performed her work in Philadelphia, San Francisco, New Jersey, and New York. Nicole was first published in *The Rutherford Red Wheelbarrow* and would like to thank William Carlos Williams for the inspiration.

Don Zirilli

Don Zirilli is the editor of *Now Culture* (nowcukture.com). He owns a black wheelbarrow and a green wheelbarrow.